# INNOCENT VICTIMS

# INNOCENT VICTIMS

## Thomas Whiteman, Ph.D.

**THOMAS NELSON PUBLISHERS**
Nashville

Published in Nashville, Tennessee, by Oliver-Nelson Books, a division of Thomas Nelson, Inc., Publishers, and distributed in Canada by Lawson Falle, Ltd., Cambridge, Ontario.

The Bible version used in this publication is THE NEW KING JAMES VERSION. Copyright © 1979, 1980, 1982, Thomas Nelson, Inc., Publishers.

Printed in the United States of America.

Library of Congress Cataloging-in-Publication Data

Whiteman, Tom.
Innocent victims : understanding the needs & fears of your children / Thomas Whiteman.
p.   cm.
ISBN 0-8407-9172-0 (pbk.)
1. Children of divorced parents—United States—Psychology.
2. Single-parent family—United States.   I. Title.
HQ777.5.W53    1992
306.89—dc20                                                        92-30229
                                                                              CIP

2   3   4   5   6   —   97   96   95

This book is dedicated to the more than
five hundred single parents, and their
children, whose stories provided the impetus
for this book. It is their stories and their
experiences that will be shared here, and it was
for their sakes that this book was written. It is
hoped that our combined efforts will help to
alleviate some of the negative consequences of
divorce for the tens of thousands of families
in crisis who will pick up this book
and read their stories.

# CONTENTS

## SECTION III: HELPING YOUR CHILDREN

# INTRODUCTION

This book has grown out of an obvious need—a need that is evidenced in our city streets, our jails, and among our homeless, but also in our private schools, our churches, and in the nicest of neighborhoods. The need has been felt dramatically by all those who have watched as their children have reacted to the disruption of the family. It is the need for early intervention in the lives of those who are experiencing the breakup of their families. This was specifically brought to my attention quite vividly through my involvement with the Fresh Start Seminars.

Fresh Start Seminars began as a program for separated and divorced adults, to help them grow beyond their pain to a point of acceptance in an entirely new lifestyle. The leadership team soon learned that one cannot effectively address the needs of the separated and divorced without helping them with their children. Many of the "single again" listed as their first concern the emotional survival of their children. Yet as I listened to their stories, I became aware that many well–educated adults seemed to be doing it all wrong when it came to the needs of their children. I am writing this book in the hope of reaching as many of these parents as possible.

The statistics for children of divorce are discouraging. Yet I believe that early intervention can make an enormous difference. Timely information and support, for both children and parents, can lessen the negative effects of divorce.

In 1982, at the outset of the Fresh Start Divorce Recovery Program, parents by the dozens asked me: "When are you going to do something for our children?" Their greatest concern was for their kids. I could hear their emotional cry for help, yet I felt ill-prepared to do anything. I remember thinking that someone should sponsor a program for these children. As I observed, listened, and read research on the effects of divorce on children, the burden began to touch me.

Having worked in the Philadelphia School District for six years as a psychologist, I was very aware of the needs of divorced kids. About 80 percent of the students referred to me for emotional or educational problems came from single–parent families. To address this need within the school system I started some small–group counseling sessions specifically designed for the children of divorce. Through these groups, I discovered just how necessary it was for these students to learn that there were other kids who were faced with similar difficulties; those who were dealing with insecurity, emotional pain, and the embarrassment of coming from a family where Dad wasn't around or Mom just didn't care. The opportunity to talk about their experiences and to encourage one another proved to be therapeutic for them, and provided me with early insights into the needs of such children. In retrospect, I can see how I was being prepared for a ministry to children of divorce that would grow far beyond the Philadelphia area.

My next attempt to offer a program for children of divorce was during the Sunday School hour at the church where I was attending. I felt that the church was the ideal place for such a program because: 1) it typically addresses the needs of the traditional family to the exclusion of others; 2) the church includes the potential for whole–family participation; 3) the church should be a place of hope and healing, particularly to those who are struggling with difficult life issues.

The first week the class met with only eight students. It was difficult for them to come because they felt embarrassed, and believed they were the only ones who did not fit into the Christian family stereotype. Some had no father at home. Others had a mother who had abandoned the family. Somehow it did not seem spiritual to admit to such problems at home. Eventually, the students began to open up and trust one another. They became a significant support group, and were a tremendous encouragement to me and to each other.

This class for the young victims of divorce grew in number. As it did, the students began to talk about other kids within their community who had no safe place in which to talk openly about what they were experiencing. They asked, "Why don't we do something for these children of divorce?" This was the very question their parents had been asking me for years. The students pointed to the Divorce Recovery Seminar offered by Fresh Start for adults, and wondered why they couldn't have a similar seminar for kids. So in 1987 we sponsored the first Fresh Start for Kids seminar at the Church of the Saviour in Wayne, Pennsylvania. Over fifty children attended.

Today Fresh Start Seminars and Fresh Start for Kids Seminars are held in many locations throughout the United States and two foreign countries. We attempt to conduct the weekend seminars simultaneously so that entire families can come together for a time of insight and healing. Brochures and other materials are available through the Fresh Start office at 63 Chestnut Road, Paoli, PA 19301.

This book is a direct outgrowth of that first seminar, and the others that followed. It is designed to provide single parents and other concerned individuals with helpful suggestions and new insights to help children who are experiencing the breakup of their families. With support and guidance, you can make a difference in the lives of these children, the truly innocent victims of divorce.

SECTION 1

# UNDERSTANDING
# YOUR CHILDREN

# THROUGH THE
# EYES OF A CHILD

I will never forget Eddie Hyser. I was in fourth grade in a typical suburban classroom. It seemed as though each of the girls had long blonde locks of hair. Each of the boys had straight brown bangs hanging over their eyes. We all waited anxiously for lunch, or recess, . . . or summer! It must have been a simpler time, because I don't ever remember hearing about child abuse, child pornography, or even custody battles. Each student came from the typical American home: two parents, a station wagon, and a safe neighborhood to play in. That is . . . except for Eddie.

Eddie was different. Whenever there was a problem in class, whenever something went wrong, or whenever there was a fight at the playground, we knew that somehow Eddie was involved. We liked Eddie well enough, but it seemed like one by one each of us would get in trouble when we played with Eddie. So one by one we either drew away from him or were forbidden by our parents to play with him.

I remember the time I got in trouble playing with Eddie and a couple of other boys. Someone was fooling with matches and somehow a fire got started. The fire burned a small field and the back of a garage. The police came and, of course, Eddie received primary blame. I got into trouble as well, but what I remember most was being told that I shouldn't play with Eddie. He was a "bad influence."

I don't know what happened to Eddie Hyser. I know that he was different from the rest of us. He acted differently and came from a different kind of home than we did. You see, Eddie came from a broken home.

It seems strange to look back on that experience and realize Eddie was the only classmate I can remember who came from a single–parent family. Now I know that statistically there must have been many more families like Eddie's, just as I know there must have been child abuse, family violence, and custody battles. Yet I was completely unaware of their existence. It wasn't until I became an adult that I began to realize the extent of the problem that children have as a result of their family breakups.

My childhood took place in a different day and age. Divorce rates were much lower, and for those who were going through divorce there was a greater need to keep silent because of society's stigma on them. Today, however, the problem of divorce is more prevalent. Yet what many people don't realize is that in the minds of children, the stigma and trauma of divorce are as real as ever.

Recent estimates tell us that one million children go through the experience of a family breakup each year. Just under one–half of all marriages will end in divorce. About 40 percent of all American children will spend some time in a single–parent family before they reach the age of eighteen. Growing up in a divorced home is not a rare occurrence, but rather the norm for today's society.

Today we no longer call these families "broken homes." The negative connotation and implied failure are too obvious. Instead, we call them single–parent families. But the emotional effects are still the same.

As prevalent as divorce has become, in the eyes of children, they still feel as if they are the only ones going through such trauma. Why do they feel this way? There are several reasons.

First, most people, and especially children, don't think about the problem of divorce until it affects them directly.

Second, children are egocentric, which means they only pay attention to things that affect them. They tend to be selfish, only dealing with life's circumstances as they affect their own lives. If they are not faced with the problem of divorce, they give it little or no thought.

The third reason children feel like they are the

only ones going through such difficulties is because most kids, and people in general, tend to keep to themselves the emotional hurts and trauma of a family breakup. Whether society causes it or not, people still feel the stigma of failure attached to the divorce experience, so they do not talk about what they are going through. Most children are taught to keep family matters private, so they do not talk in school about what's going on at home.

While working in a school system, I was surprised to see how many students kept significant secrets from their classmates and teachers. Their elaborate schemes would include lying about weekend trips they had supposedly made with their fantasy families, and making up wild stories about why both of their parents had not been able to attend a parent/teacher conference. But their hiding of the truth only thwarted opportunities that might have been available to them; such as, support groups within the school, or a classmate who could empathize with their experience.

# AN OVERVIEW

This book is divided into three sections. Section I, "Understanding Your Children" (chapters 1 and 2), is designed to help you understand how children of divorce are different from divorcing adults. The focus of the second section, "Your Children's Reaction" (chapters 3 through 7), is to examine how children of divorce are different from children of intact families. This will be done in a way that explores both short–term and long–term reactions to the divorce experience. Section III, "Helping Your Children" (chapters 8 through 10), will provide specific guidelines as to how you can minimize the differences between your children and children from intact families, and how to help your children recover into new and healthy lifestyles.

The appendix is designed to provide you with a list of additional resources, dealing with specific issues. Hopefully, the recommended books on each topic will be a valuable resource. All books referred to in the text are listed in the appendix.

There are times when the information given might be difficult to hear, yet I want to emphasize that there is hope. I wish that each of you could meet some of the children and teenagers whom I interviewed in preparation for this book. Some had recently experienced a parental breakup, while others had been in single–parent or blended families for years. What I observed, I will not forget. They are some of the most loving, responsible, and sensitive kids I have ever met. It is easier to overlook all of the negative statistics when you can sit down and talk with any of these students face to face.

As many of you read this book, you will feel great frustration with the suggestions that you know are beyond your ability to implement; or perhaps it is now too late to do them. Parents literally can torment themselves over circumstances that are completely out of their control. If you are to survive as a single parent you need to adopt the attitude that I believe is best expressed in the Serenity Prayer, which has been popularized by Alcoholics Anonymous.

"God, grant me the serenity to accept the things I cannot change, the courage to change the things I can, and the wisdom to know the difference."

As you read this book you must keep this prayer in mind. There are changes which you can make that will have a very positive impact on your children. There are other circumstances that might be quite negative, over which you have no control. It is these things that you must let go of, except as a matter for prayer. The really difficult part, and that which requires the greatest wisdom, is knowing which things you need to change, and which you should leave with God.

Perhaps a simple example would be most helpful. A common problem for divorcing parents, yet an important factor, is the parents' attitude toward their children and toward each other. You *can* control your own attitude, but you can't control the other parent. Many parents expend a lot of energy trying to get the other parent to be more loving or responsible when the kids are with him or her. Yet this may only worsen the problem, since your ex-spouse usually resents your input, while at the same time you are only frustrating yourself. The frustration toward your ex can't help but be reflected onto your kids, who now view you as too busy with your own problems to be accessible to them.

The alternative, and more helpful, solution is to pray for the other parent's relationship with the children, while you concentrate on loving the kids as best as you can. Hugs, listening to them, companionship at sporting events or concerts, etc., are obvious expressions of support that many single parents overlook. They might be too busy thinking about what the other parent should be doing differently, or perhaps they are wishing *they* were supported.

# UNDERSTANDING YOUR CHILDREN

In this first section of the book, which includes chapters 1 and 2, I have sought to show how your children's reactions to divorce are different from your own. When we try to understand why children act and react the way they do in response to divorce, we must first understand the different ways adults and children think. Many people mistakenly think of children as miniature adults. The truth of the matter is that children think and act very differently from ourselves. To effectively help children of divorce we must take these differences seriously and seek to understand how they affect our children's reactions.

Many parents believe that they need only to love and nurture their children, and that everything will turn out okay. As important as these ingredients are, it is impossible to truly love and nurture someone you don't understand. It takes a special effort to see the divorce situation through the eyes of a child. This is emphasized by Dr. Stuart Berger in his book *Divorce Without Victims* (p. 16):

> It is absolutely essential for the parent to realize that until the child reaches young adulthood, his view of the world and the people around him is very different from the adult's. Even the teenager who appears full grown in so many ways, is somewhat at the mercy of his continuing physical and emotional development. Your behavior toward your child, whatever his age, during the period of parental separation and divorce, must take into account his particular stage of development.

There are a number of important concepts for adults to understand about how children think, if they are to help them through the trauma of divorce. In the next chapter we will look at a few of these key concepts. We will examine the ways in which the mind of the child differs from the mind of the adult.

# CHAPTER SUMMARY

In this first chapter we have taken a look back and seen how attitudes toward divorce and children of divorce have changed. Yet there is still evidence of a significant stigma, perhaps one that the participants place on themselves, when families break up. Children who experience the divorce of their parents tend to feel very alone and different—different from other children, and different from their parents. We have outlined how these differences will be covered within the first two sections of the book. Helping your children overcome these differences, and the negative emotions that go with them, will be the topic of the third section.

# WHY DON'T WE THINK ALIKE?

If asked, "Why don't our kids think the way we do?", many of us would respond that it is because we are older and wiser than our children. While this is probably true, this explanation doesn't do justice to the complex developmental differences between children and adults. In this chapter we will take a closer look at some key differences. These include the difference between the concrete thinking of children and the abstract reasoning of adults, the egocentric thinking of children and adult awareness of others, the magical thinking of children and an adult sense of reality.

## CONCRETE THINKING

At the age of seven, Kathy's parents were separated. When she spoke to me in counseling, she revealed that her father left the home because he and her mother had a fight. In reality, Dad was involved with another woman, and was planning a divorce so that he could marry his new lover. To Kathy, her parents had merely had a disagreement and would eventually make up. She explained that she had had squabbles with her best friend, but that they always worked things out after a period of not speaking to each other.

Kathy continued that she knew her father was going to move back to their home soon, because he had said that he still loved her very much. "Everyone knows that you don't leave someone you love," reasoned Kathy. "Both of my parents have always taught me that."

For Kathy, what she concluded was a combination of what she had been told and what she had experienced firsthand. To children this is their reality, and this is an example of concrete thinking. As adults we have the ability to think abstractly. This is our ability to go beyond a specific situation and to make conclusions that we have not been taught. For example, if Kathy were older (perhaps twelve, depending on her developmental maturity), she may have concluded that even when people love each other they don't always act in loving ways. Or, she may have figured out that people don't break off their marriages because of a fight, and that there must be more going on than Dad is admitting.

Another example of children's concrete thinking is found in the way they view morality. Children usually begin to view right and wrong according to whatever their parents teach them.

They can't reason for themselves yet. Later in life they begin to modify their parents' views according to their own experiences, combined with input from teachers and friends. This "new morality" is merely a black–and–white view of what is right and wrong, based on experiences. There is a general inability to deal with any "gray" areas, and therefore, children tend to be legalistic.

As children mature, so does their ability to reason abstractly. They begin to understand the intentions and motives of others. They become more flexible and understanding of individual differences. They gain the ability to empathize with others even though they have never been through similar situations. Let me illustrate this development through some examples.

Why don't you steal? Your earliest memory as a child probably dictated that you shouldn't steal because your mom or dad said that it was bad. Perhaps later you observed other kids stealing toys and getting away with it. But just before you concluded that it was okay to steal, you saw someone get caught. So you learned that you shouldn't steal because you would be punished if you got caught. Hopefully, by the time you reach adulthood you begin to realize there are many other reasons for not stealing, even if you know there is no chance you would get caught.

It is interesting to note that some adults never reach this final stage of reasoning. They go through life believing that it's okay to steal as long as you don't get caught. This is not only tragic, but it also indicates an immature or dys-functional development of their moral reasoning.

In terms of the divorce experience, Kathy would be a good example. At age six, when her father first announced that he was leaving, she couldn't believe it, because she always heard from him that he loved her and would never leave. When he actually moved out, Kathy, at age seven, was convinced that Dad left because of a fight, since that was what was going on while he was packing his bags.

In the absence of any other information, Kathy continued to believe this for several years. She thought her mom was good because she stayed at home, and her dad was bad because he left. As she saw her dad with another woman, she was jealous of his attention, but did not think much of it; that is, until she was about ten or so. Then she began to make the inference that her dad may have left *because* of this other woman. Now she was really angry at both her dad and this new woman, who was now her stepmother.

As a teenager, Kathy did not support her dad's actions, but began to be more sympathetic and understanding toward him. She concluded, "Re-lationships are very complicated, and I'm sure my dad had his reasons for doing what he did. I know he didn't *want* to hurt us the way he did."

Concrete thinking deals entirely with the here and now. It is not concerned with consequences or intentions, nor does it take into account the feelings of others. Divorce is viewed in terms of how it affects me.

"My family broke up because of me." "I'm the only one going through this." "What am I going to do now?" I have heard these phrases again and again from the children of divorce. Many children will not understand that there are other kids going through the same trauma until they see them and talk to them personally. This reinforces the need for children's support groups.

In the transitional period, somewhere between the years of twelve and twenty, teens gradually develop abstract reasoning skills. Divorce tends to delay this maturation process, since children, when they feel threatened, will usually retreat to a more comfortable, earlier learned stage of response. This is known as regression.

I remember Peter. He first came to see me as a ten–year–old fifth grade student who was showing signs of emotional difficulties. His teacher referred him to me because he was withdrawn and depressed. After hearing this description, I remembered how surprised I was when, after the first few minutes of our meeting, Peter began to open up and pour out his emotional concerns. He described his parents' separation, which occurred when he was about five years old. He had many questions about it then, but didn't know how to ask them. He didn't remember any explanation as to why his dad left.

For five years Peter lived with many unanswered questions. Since explanation and counsel had not been given, he concluded that he must have been pretty bad to cause his father to leave. Teachers and fellow students had no idea what was wrong because Peter never talked about it. He had become emotionally isolated.

Peter explained to me that he felt different because he was the only one in the school who had no father at home. His emotional isolation is evident. Here was a boy in an inner city school, with over fifty percent of its population coming from single-parent families, and Peter had no idea that other kids were also struggling through the painful breakup of their homes.

Peter's recovery was fairly rapid once we got to the heart of the problem and began to address the issues. I asked Peter to go home and ask his mom why she and his dad had broken up. In the meantime I called his mother and advised her to answer his questions as openly and honestly as she could, giving concrete examples as to why the marriage could not work. She was surprised by my request, since this had happened five years earlier. In her mind it was all over and done with. What was settled in her adult mind was far from settled in her son's.

I started a counseling group in Peter's class for those who were from single-parent families. They openly shared their embarrassment at feeling alone and different. By their presence they provided concrete evidence of the fact that others close by were sharing the same experience.

Before long, Peter began to feel more a part of

his class. He no longer felt different or unusual. He began to speak up and interact with his class-mates. He also learned from his mom that he was not to blame for his dad's leaving. Peter began to feel better about himself.

Divorcing parents should never assume that their kids will figure out what went wrong. They will need concrete explanations. This is one rea-son many kids have an especially difficult time accepting separation or divorce when there was little or no observable fighting. I'm not suggesting that couples should *try* to fight in front of their children. But when there has been little concrete evidence of a problem, it is no wonder the kids have a difficult time accepting the marital breakup. Children need explanations and con-crete examples that they will be able to under-stand.

Children will generally relate the family breakup to whatever disruptive event happened most recently in the home. This is another exam-ple of concrete thinking. The younger the chil-dren, the greater the tendency to react in this way, since their memories are not well developed.

When Sally, a seven–year–old second grader, brought home a bad report card, her parents yelled at her. This led to a big fight between Mom and Dad, which culminated in her father's storm-ing out of the home. It was not surprising when Sally informed me that her father left and eventu-ally divorced her mom because Sally had gotten bad grades.

I recall the six–year–old boy who informed me that his father left because his mother made the wrong thing for dinner. You can imagine what happened in that home just before Dad walked out the door.

These are not isolated examples. Research indicates that more than half of all children and teens who experience the breakup of their families believe that they were at least partially to blame. This phenomenon is due, I believe, to a combination of two factors: concrete thinking and egocentrism, which will be covered in the next section.

As parents, what can we do about our children's concrete thinking? You cannot hurry children's emotional or mental development. Like physical maturation, emotional development is generally predetermined and will only occur as a result of natural processes. However, divorce does tend to cause children to regress in their development. This is not because their maturity process is slower, but because insecure kids will tend to do and think things that are familiar and comfortable to them. They are not willing to stretch themselves with new challenges when their world is falling apart.

Fortunately, the developmental process balances out as children's lives begin to stabilize. As parents, you need to try to provide as stable an environment as you can, as quickly as you can after the breakup of the family. Stability—not finding another spouse—should be your number one priority.

Help your children by giving honest, clear information. Your children's questions deserve concrete answers. These are the only kind of answers your children will understand. A direct question, "Why did Daddy leave?" deserves a direct response: "Because when Daddy and Mommy are together we fight a lot and that makes us both very unhappy." Or, "Because Daddy loves someone else and wants to be with her." Or maybe, "I'm sorry but I just don't know why Daddy left." If that's the truth, then that's what your answer should be. If you do tell your children you don't know why Dad or Mom left, you'd better discover an answer as soon as possible, and then let your children know the truth.

## EGOCENTRIC THINKING

Kids are basically selfish. Most people are aware of that fact. It is a normal and necessary stage of development for all children to be egocentric. This means that children go through a time when they believe that the whole world revolves around them. For example, very young children believe that the entire family eats at 5:30 P.M. because *they* are hungry. Children are not capable of thinking any other way. And the younger the children, the more egocentric they are likely to be.

When my daughter was one year old, she believed the only reason that Mommy and Daddy existed was to satisfy her every desire. She whined when she wanted to eat, and again when she was tired. If you try to tell a one– or two–year–old, "I'm sorry. I can't pick you up right now because I'm busy," it probably won't get you very far.

Children retain some degree of egocentric thinking well into adolescence. They gradually change because of their increasing awareness of others and their growing ability to understand abstractly other people's point of view.

Let me share an example of how one's ability to think abstractly begins to change egocentricity. Did you ever wonder why elementary and junior high kids can be so cruel to their classmates, particularly to those who are different or handicapped in some way? This is an example of egocentric *and* concrete thinking. "It doesn't hurt *me.*" Or, "I don't care how it makes *them* feel." Children are generally unable to put themselves abstractly into another person's shoes and empathize with how they must feel. So parents should not expect their children to empathize with them over their divorce. Children can feel only their own pain.

As a parent you try to explain over and over why picking on others is wrong, or try to have your children understand a different point of view. Yet it seems like you're wasting your breath. Then gradually, and independently of your efforts, your children enter high school and begin to feel empathy or compassion for others who are suffering. Teasing of others dissipates to a point where many young adults will begin to reach out to others less fortunate than themselves.

It is unfortunate but true that many teenagers, and some adults, continue to be thoroughly self–centered well beyond the age where they should know better. This is usually not a reflection of their inability to understand how others feel (unless they are developmentally or mentally retarded). Rather, it is more a reflection of bad habits, a family pattern, or a personality trait. The difference between adults and children is that children are not capable of adult thinking and relating.

How does egocentric thinking relate to the divorce experience? Divorce tends to make this egocentric thinking become more pronounced and obvious. Even the most giving adults will retreat emotionally, and immediately think only of self–protection when they go through a divorce. Likewise, children think only in terms of how all of this is going to affect them.

One teenager told me, "Here I am, just getting to the point where I'm ready to start dating and my mom and dad pull this. How am I ever going to bring someone home to meet my parents when they're not even together?"

Another student said, "Now that this has happened, what are we going to do about my birthday party next year?"

Egocentric thinking may cause children and teenagers to become angry with the custodial parent. They expect their parent to do something about the separation or divorce. And they may be too self–centered to realize that their parent is powerless to change the circumstances. That is why a young mother who has been abandoned by her husband can still be blamed by her children for "making Dad go away." Egocentric thinking in children of divorce can produce painful situations, but parents should remember that this is children's nature, not malicious behavior.

Another byproduct of egocentric thinking is that children begin to overestimate their own importance. They cannot imagine anything happening that they did not somehow cause. This is one more reason why so many children of divorce believe they were somehow to blame for their parents' breakup. In the mind of the child, if everything revolves around me, then it is logical to assume that Mom or Dad left *because* of me.

For this reason it is extremely important for you to constantly reassure your children that they had nothing to do with the breakup of the family. *Don't assume that they know this. Don't assume they will ask questions if they don't know this.* Continue to reassure them as they grow and develop that they were not the cause of the breakup. They need to hear this over and over, until they are mature enough to truly comprehend what they have been through.

You may ask yourself, "Why should I bother to explain such complex matters to my children if they do not have the capacity to understand such things?" The answer is because someday they will.

Each night, as I put my daughter to bed, I tell her that I love her. Does a two–year–old know what that means? Does she understand the meaning of love? Your children hear the information over and over and gain a superficial understanding of what your statement of love means. As they get older, the depth of the meaning of your words becomes increasingly clear, until one day your children finally realize the significance of what you have been telling them all along.

So it is with children's understanding of the issues surrounding their parents' divorce. Each new stage of development brings with it not only new understandings, but new questions, which previously had not been considered.

## MAGICAL THINKING

As children, we always enjoyed a nursery rhyme or a short children's tale. One reason we enjoyed them is because the characters always lived happily ever after. This happily–ever–after thinking corresponds to our childhood magical thinking. Children believe that somehow everything is going to turn out okay because they wish it.

I recall the freckle–faced six–year–old boy in my office who told me that he felt badly because he wished his father were dead. I asked him why that made him feel badly. He responded that by wishing his father were dead, he was afraid that his dad would really die.

At the time I thought it unusual for this boy to believe that he could wish his father to death. Yet in terms of magical thinking it makes perfect sense. By thinking it, the boy believed he could bring it to pass.

Quoting from Dr. Stuart Berger's *Divorce Without Victims* (p. 21):

> Magical thinking is a result in a sense of the child's perception that he is all powerful, that he causes all things to happen. Such thinking can lead not only to feelings of omnipotence, but to guilt and distress on the child's part. An understanding of magical thinking will help you to comprehend your child's sometimes puzzling reactions to divorce.

It is this magical thinking that causes most children of divorce to continue believing that their parents will eventually get back together, even after years of separation. I have observed this phenomenon numerous times, and research has borne out the fact that most kids hang on to an unrealistic fantasy that their parents will someday be reunited.

Magical thinking is most pronounced in children between the ages of four and eight. The combination of egocentric thinking and magical thinking leads to an inescapable conclusion: "My parents will get back together because that's what *I* want."

Billy was only seven, but was very mature because of what he had experienced. On a number of occasions, by the age of four, he had witnessed his mother being beaten. One time he had even called the police, and had watched his father being taken away in handcuffs. Even though his parents had been separated off and on over the past three years, he was surprised when his father left for the last time.

When Billy came to talk with me, he revealed much anger and resentment toward his father. In great detail he recalled incident after incident in which his abusive father had either hurt someone or broken something. Yet when Billy talked about the future, it always included his dad moving home and interacting with the family in a healthy manner.

Was this merely a childhood fantasy, or did Billy really believe that his miracle was going to happen? Young children have a difficult time separating fact and fantasy. And adults have a difficult time knowing what a child is thinking. Certainly, for the child younger than six, there is a real belief that "Mommy will remarry Daddy and we will live happily together." After all, they believe that Santa and the Easter Bunny are coming as well.

After the age of six, children gradually begin to understand make–believe and fantasy. However, many still think that if they wish for something hard enough they can probably make it happen. This is a supposition that is supported by many of our favorite children's fairy tales.

As they develop and become less egocentric, children learn that they can't control adults nor make things happen by sheer will. They cannot make Tinkerbell live again by wishing very hard. Yet some children of divorce continue to hold on to the hopeless fantasy well into their teenage years that their parents will reunite.

Patty was fourteen when she first came to see me for counseling. Her parents had been divorced since she was five. When she was younger, Patty used to see her father every other weekend. However, when she was eight her father remarried and moved about fifty miles away. From that time on, she saw her father only during major holidays, and for two weeks in the summer. As is usually the case, Patty did not like her stepmother, whom she always referred to as her stepmonster.

This is how Patty described her magical thinking:

> When I was younger I always dreamed about the day when my mom and dad would get back together and we could be a family again. Then when my dad got married to that witch, I felt like she had taken him away from us. Whenever I went over for a visit, I have to admit that I was kind of a brat. I sort

of wanted my stepmonster to be miserable, so that she would leave and then my mom and dad could get back together again. Now I realize that that will probably never happen. In fact, Mom told me that she and Dad wouldn't get married again even if he and my stepmom got a divorce. Still, there are a lot of days that I think I wouldn't have had so many problems if only my parents had stuck together.

Even divorced adults can retain some aspects of magical thinking. They live with the expectation that their ex will return, repent of all wrongdoing, and beg to be taken back. Or some may live for the day that Mr. or Ms. Right will come along and rescue them from a lonely life.

Is this just wishful thinking? Perhaps. But there is just enough little kid in all of us to keep our hopes alive. We need to be careful that we face our fantasies for what they are. Otherwise we will be left even more disillusioned, lonely, and despairing. (See the appendix on remarriage.)

## CHAPTER SUMMARY

In this chapter we have examined some of the differences between children's and adult's thinking. In particular, we have explored the ways in which concrete thinking, egocentric thinking, and magical thinking combine to cause children of divorce to feel alone, to focus on *their* heartaches only, to blame themselves for some aspect of the breakup, and to hold on to the belief that some day their parents will get back together.

In the next section we will begin to look at the reactions of children who are experiencing the breakup of their parents. Now that we better understand the way our children think, we will be able to view their reactions through the eyes of a child.

# YOUR
# CHILDREN'S
# REACTION

# TYPICAL
# REACTIONS

Bobby was sound asleep when his mother shook him to get him up. "Get up, Bobby! Grab your blankie and teddy bear. We're going bye–bye."

Bobby, who was only five years old, quickly grabbed his things as his mother whisked him away in the middle of the night. He remembered very little beyond that point, as he drifted in and out of sleep. His mother took him downstairs, loaded him into a car full of family belongings, and drove off to Bobby's grandmother's house at the other end of town.

When Bobby woke up the following morning and saw that he was at his grandmother's, he realized that he hadn't been dreaming about the night before. He was glad to be at his grandmom's, but was a little confused as to why they had left home so abruptly.

Bobby asked his mother all kinds of questions as they sat around the breakfast table. "Where is

Daddy? What are we going to do today? When are we going home?"

His mother's evasiveness and tendency to change the subject only caused Bobby to be more confused and curious.

Later that same day, as Bobby was being put to bed in his grandmother's spare room, he once again asked his mother, "Where's Daddy?" and "When are we going home?"

His mother looked down at the ground and said, "I don't know where Daddy is, and I don't know when we're going home."

Bobby, who was pretty smart for his age, was now very confused. He knew that there was something wrong. Mom was acting funny. Grandmom and Grandpop were acting differently. This wasn't like the typical visit to Grandmom's house. Daddy wasn't with them.

He soon began to wonder, "Did I do something wrong? I wonder if Dad is mad at me?"

"Well," he reasoned, "at least I haven't been yelled at or punished, so maybe everything will be back to normal tomorrow."

The days came and went, sometimes seeming almost normal. But most days Bobby wondered, "What is going on with my family? Why isn't Daddy around?"

The more he asked questions, the more his grandparents and his mother seemed to avoid giving answers.

Then one day, after more days than Bobby could count (actually it was several months), his mother came to him and said, "Bobby, sit down. We need to talk." Mom began to explain that she and his dad were not going to live together any more. She talked about their fighting, about them not being in love any more, but Bobby didn't understand any of that. He only remembered that his mother said that he and his dad were not going to live together. Oh, he liked his grandparents all right. And he liked living there with his mother. But he didn't understand why he, Mom, and Dad couldn't live together again in their old house.

He had lots of questions, but didn't know how to ask them. So Bobby only nodded his head, and ran off to play. He was still a little confused as to what was going to happen to him.

His mother, on the other hand, thought that things had gone really well. She had avoided saying anything to Bobby up until that point because she didn't want to hurt him. Besides, for a long time she wasn't sure whether her separation from her husband was going to be permanent.

Now, after almost three months at Grandmom's house, Bobby's mother had come to the decision that she was going to seek a divorce. She had talked to her parents and had sought counsel from the pastor at the church. She finally concluded that she could no longer live a lie. The hardest part for her was telling Bobby. But once she made up her mind, she knew it had to be done.

When Bobby didn't object, cry, or react traumatically to this difficult news, Bobby's mom assumed that he had taken it fairly well. She had no idea what was going on inside the mind of her child.

As the months progressed, Bobby's mother became more and more preoccupied with her own problems. She had reestablished contact with her husband, most of which was unpleasant. They were discussing lawyers, custody arrangements, and financial settlements, which all brought about increased stress. One bright spot, however, was the observation that Bobby seemed to be fine. He had found a few friends in his new neighborhood, and seemed perfectly content with the new living arrangement.

Bobby's needs and his adjustment became secondary to the questions his mother was asking herself; such as: "Where are we going to live? How can I support a household as a single parent? Will I ever be happy again?" Bobby's mother comforted herself with the thought that at least her child was doing okay.

That consolation didn't last very long. Bobby's mother had just worked through an arrangement where Bobby could visit his dad on alternating weekends, when things began to change.

Bobby was excited when his mom first told him about the visit to his dad's. However, within hours after that, he began to behave differently. At first Bobby acted very cold toward his mom. She just thought that he must have a lot on his mind. But soon this distance turned into overt anger.

This was displayed as temper tantrums, talking back, and refusing to fulfill even the simplest responsibility. To make matters even worse, it seemed as though each time Bobby returned from a visit with his dad, he demonstrated even more anger toward his mom.

At school, Bobby was progressing in first grade. However, as visitation with his dad continued, his grades began to slip. At a subsequent parent/teacher conference, Bobby's mother was surprised to learn that her son was showing signs of anger in school. He was fighting in the schoolyard, picking on other kids, and displaying a bad attitude toward schoolwork.

For Bobby's mom, this was the last straw. She decided to send him to the school guidance counselor so that she could gain some new insights into Bobby's problem. She assumed that his problems had something to do with his father, since she hadn't had any trouble with him before the weekend visits began.

A few months went by, along with several visits to the counselor. Bobby began to show gradual improvement in his behavior. His temper tantrums lessened, and the school reported fewer problems. His grades, however, were still low. He was described as being very distracted.

Bobby's counselor reported that he was opening up in the sessions and sharing his concerns over his parents' breakup. The counselor indicated that the visits to Dad were not the cause of his problems, but that his insecurity over seeing his father merely triggered a reaction.

A year after the breakup of Bobby's family, he was showing fewer and fewer signs of anger, but now seemed more sad and withdrawn. His mother noticed him crying alone in bed a few times. He also seemed very distant and withdrawn whenever his weekend visits were approaching. She assumed that Bobby would work through these problems. After all, he was in counseling, and she had her own concerns to work through.

Bobby's schoolwork remained poor, but at least he was passing. His teachers now described him as being withdrawn and uninvolved in classroom activities. Most affected were his reading level and handwriting skills, which seemed to regress as he approached the end of first grade.

As time passed, Bobby showed improvement, but would revert to his withdrawn or sullen behavior around holidays, or any kind of special family event. He seemed very sensitive to change and was quick to display anger or sorrow.

This emotional roller coaster did not begin to level off until about three years after the separation of Bobby's parents. They were now divorced and there was a consistent visitation arrangement, which seemed to be working well. Bobby's mom and dad were even talking to each other more civilly now. The only change in this slow and steady growth of improvement was when Bobby's mother went out on her first date.

Bobby, who was now eight, acted horribly that whole week. And when the person came over to pick up his mom, Bobby was at his all–time worst. He acted rudely and refused to even speak to the man. Throughout the following week, Bobby seemed very angry and rude toward his mother. It wasn't until weeks later that Bobby finally came to his mom and asked, "When are you and Dad going to get back together?" His mother used this opportunity to explain once again to Bobby the finality of their divorce and to reassure him of their commitment to his well-being.

Today, Bobby is in high school. He has the same insecurities and struggles that most teenagers experience. It's difficult for his mother to determine how many of his problems are due to the broken home, and how many are part of normal teenage development.

Bobby has a fairly good relationship with his mom, but rarely sees his dad due to their typically busy schedules. Bobby's grades are back to normal, and he is fairly involved in normal high school activities. The only remnants of his parents' divorce seem to be those nagging questions that he still struggles with, but rarely talks about. These questions include:

- I wonder if my parents will ever get back together again?
- I wonder if I did something to cause my parents to get their divorce?
- Does my dad really love me? And if he

does, why doesn't he visit very often? Is he
really too busy?
• Why couldn't Mom stick with Dad just for
my sake?
• I wonder what kind of parent and husband
I will be, considering the fact that I've
never really lived in a "normal" family.

Even though most of these questions have been
answered, Bobby still has them, nagging at the
back of his mind, creating insecurity and hesi-
tancy about trusting in relationships.

## THREE MAJOR CATEGORIES

Bobby's example might seem like an isolated
case, yet it is fairly typical of those who work
through their parents' divorce in a healthy way.
A number of studies have demonstrated that
children have similar patterns in reacting to
their parents' divorce (see Joan Kelly's article,
"Longer-Term Adjustment in Children of Divorce," in the *Journal of Family Psychology*, De-
cember, 1988). These reactions can be divided
into three general categories.

The first category, which includes approximately one–third (about 27 percent) of the children of divorce, contains those children who
come through their parents' breakup in a fairly
healthy manner, as in the case of Bobby. They go
through the normal grieving process, experienc-

ing denial, anger, and depression. Usually within two years, they reach a point of acceptance. This acceptance seems contingent on their parents' ability to work through an amicable settlement. This usually includes a reduced number of disruptions following the divorce, such as remarriage, a major change in lifestyle, or inconsistent visitation.

Typically, there are points of disruption beyond the two–year adjustment period, such as when Mom or Dad might start dating, or maybe even get remarried. Yet this one–third of the children of divorce demonstrate a fairly healthy adjustment. In fact, two years after the divorce, this group cannot be distinguished from other children whose parents have remained together.

A counselor, or someone very close to children in this group, might recognize the fact that many of them still have persistent questions about their parents' divorce, even five to fifteen years later. Yet to an outside observer, they seem like typical children, with the same activities, values, and concerns.

The second third of the children of divorce (approximately 34 percent) go through the typical stages of grieving, but seem to take a lot longer to go through each of the stages. In particular, they don't reach a point of acceptance within a two–year time period, but rather tend to take anywhere from three to ten years. Generally there are more boys than girls in this category, since boys tend to react more strongly and take longer to recover.

This middle group also tends to include children who have more family stresses to deal with than just their parents' divorce. These complications can include, but are not limited to:

- A major move, or major change in lifestyle, usually a drastic decrease in financial status.
- Remarriage of one of the spouses and/or the blending of families.
- Alcoholism, drug abuse, or any type of physical abuse from either parent.
- A particularly messy divorce, such as a prolonged legal battle or custody fight.

This middle category can also include children of divorce who experience delayed reactions to their parents' breakup. These children may seem fine for the first two years after their parents' separation, with little or no noticeable reaction. Yet three to five years later, with the onset of a new developmental stage, such as becoming a teenager, these kids will have more severe reactions. These might include testing limits, questioning authority, and generally distinguishing themselves as troubled youth.

The long–term effects, which last into adulthood, are much less noticeable for this group of children. They finally do make appropriate adjustments, and have fairly normal adult lives.

They do, however, show some evidence of difficulty with showing trust in relationships, and they struggle with personal insecurities. This can affect their self-image, their friendships, marriages, and the way they raise their own children. Yet research is inconclusive on these points, since it is hard to determine whether or not there is a cause and effect. In other words, we don't know how much of these long–term implications are the result of the parents' divorce, and how much would have happened anyway because of the children's personality, their genetic makeup, or other life stresses that influence development.

The final one–third of children whose parents divorce (approximately 39 percent) are those who never seem to recover from the traumatic effects of their family breakup. Their anger, depression, and general inability to accept their parents' divorce continue well into their adult lives. This can result in school failure, chronic unemployment, early marriages or an unwillingness to ever get married or have a family, inability to trust others or to establish long–term relationships. In the most extreme cases, there are higher frequencies of drug or alcohol abuse, personality disorders, and perhaps even criminal behaviors.

Mike is a good example of the child who could not adjust. Mike was twenty-seven years old when I first met him at one of our church's social functions. He was friendly, but found it difficult to participate in anything other than superficial conversation. As I tried to get to know Mike over a period of several weeks, little by little he was able to peel away the veneer and to expose more of his real self. As he did, a different person began to emerge.

I eventually recognized that Mike had a drinking problem. He had a whole other set of friends, not from the church, with whom he would get drunk, and then usually get into some type of trouble. The trouble started with rowdiness and belligerence, but all too many times evolved into fights, destruction of property, and eventual arrest.

I remember the first time I learned that he had spent the night in jail. I felt badly for him, but asked, "What's going on? How could you pick a fight with a cop?"

Mike's response was one that I later heard over and over again, each time he got into trouble. "When I was six years old my parents got a divorce. My dad took off with his secretary, and I didn't see him for three years." Mike would go on to explain how upsetting his childhood was, and how unfair it all seemed.

I remember saying, "Yes, but Mike, that was twenty years ago. Isn't it time to move on with your life?"

Mike's response to my insensitive comment was filled with anger. "You don't understand! Nobody understands what it's like. Each time I get into a fight, or take a swing at a cop, I'm getting back at my dad. . . . I'd like to kill him for what he did to me and my mom."

TYPICAL REACTIONS

That comment summed up Mike's excuse each time he was thrown in jail or sent to a drug–and–alcohol rehab center. Although I continued to reach out to Mike, he began to shut me out more and more, following the pattern of all of his relationships.

I lost touch with Mike for several years. Then I ran into him one morning in a coffee shop not too long ago. I asked him about how he was doing, and where he'd been for the past several years.

Mike proceeded to tell me that he had just gotten out of prison for a drunk–driving conviction.

Surprised by this, I asked, "How did that happen?"

Mike, who was now over thirty, recited a familiar response, "When I was six years old my parents got a divorce . . ."

It seems that Mike will never fully recover from his parents' divorce. His story, with its long–term effects, is common to almost one–third of the children of divorce.

Would Mike have had problems with drinking and self–control if his parents had never divorced? No one can really know for sure. It would seem, however, that the inclination was always there, and that the divorce was only a catalyst for the problems. No one knows what other occurrences might have set off a similar reaction, or if *any* occurrence would have triggered such an intense response.

# CHAPTER SUMMARY

In this chapter we have divided divorce reactions into three general groups. These groupings are based on research, which finds that approximately one–third of the children of divorce show little or no reaction to their parents' breakup. Yes, they do go through their own grieving, but if you were a teacher in a typical classroom, these kids would appear to be no different from your average student.

The second third are those children who seem to have a more severe reaction, but eventually (three to ten years later, depending on the age of the child) work through their grieving, and go on to live productive, healthy lives. If you were a teacher, you would notice a difference in these children, in their behaviors, emotions, or even schoolwork. But if you visited them five years later, you would see them as well–adjusted.

The final third are those children who have severe reactions and never seem to recover from their parents' divorce. Our jails and rehabilitation centers house a very high percentage of adult children of divorce, with some estimates as high as 85 percent.

The good news, however, is that two–thirds of the children of divorce work through their parents' divorce and achieve reasonably healthy adulthood. For those with children of your own, one of your greatest desires is to see your children adjust as well as they can to the stresses of the family breakup, to be within that "first third" of the children of divorce. There are many things that parents can do to help their children adjust in a positive way. Later in this book we will explore some of the ways you can help your children. But first, we will explore the feelings your children are likely to have as they initially adjust to your divorce.

# THE INITIAL
# STAGE

My summer days couldn't have been more
perfect. The iridescent sun was a perfect
match with the Caribbean blue sky. I would
be on the green grass in my bare feet, looking
up at the clear sky and think to myself how
lucky I was to have all this, and to love the
world I was living in.

At least I loved it until the night came.
That's when it would start. My siblings were
supposed to be sleeping soundly so they were
unaware of the whole nightly ordeal. But,
with me being the oldest, I heard the same
thing every night. The yelling and screaming,
the slamming of doors and chairs, and the
cries of anger. Dad would get mad and Mom
would run away sobbing with frustration. I
didn't know what to think. Was it me? Or my
brother or sister? Were we causing all this
trouble? I didn't understand; it was all so
confusing.

I would pray for some kind of change in

the situation. But I must not have prayed hard enough, because it did not change. Then came the night of real terror. There was a knock at my bedroom door. In walked my mom and dad, brother and sister. My first thought was that I had obviously done something very wrong, and so I said, "Whatever it was, I didn't do it." But instead of laughing, there was only total quiet. My dad was the one who finally broke the silence. He told us that he had something very serious to talk to us about, and we should all listen closely.

My brother, sister, and I sat frozen on the edge of the bed as my mom and dad explained to us the horrid situation. When they were done, we could only guess the problems we would have to face, and the changes we would go through in this unknown thing called divorce. My dad was the one who left the next day for an apartment. It was arranged that we would see him on the weekends.

From that day on, whenever I went outside, the sun was no longer as bright, or the sky as blue. Now reality had darkened the world around me, and I had to learn to live with the consequences of divorce.

—a fourteen–year–old girl

The initial time period, just beyond your announcement to the kids that your marriage is over, is a very critical one. In any crisis, what happens immediately after the revelation is significant. For many of you, this is in the past and it is already too late to undo some things that should not have been said or done. For others, the way this is handled is beyond your control because your former partner refuses to cooperate. Whatever the situation, the beginning of the end is for many the most difficult time.

Being awakened in the middle of the night by your parents' fighting, abruptly leaving your home and father on the eve of a special holiday, having to call the police while you watch your father beating your mother, feeling like your whole world is falling apart as you suddenly move to another town without your mother's knowledge—these are all situations that I have heard described by children of divorce. It is an extremely emotional time for all parties involved. As a parent, you want it to go as smoothly as possible for your children.

Since you are most certainly going through your own grieving process (read *The Fresh Start Divorce Recovery Workbook* by Bob Burns and Tom Whiteman for help in working through your own grieving), you may be in no condition to recognize or address the emotional needs of your children. You may not even think about their emotional needs until months later. By that time there is the chance that some initial damage has already been done. Therefore, this is a very critical time period for you to seek help from others: family, friends, a school counselor, or some other type of professional. If your family or friends are

## YOUR CHILDREN'S REACTION

as emotionally wrapped up in the problem as you are, then they may not be the best source of help.

It is also important for you to know what you can expect from your children. In terms of their reaction, you need to know what is normal and what emotional stages they will experience as time progresses.

It's just like when your children get the flu. You can see that they don't feel well and you know they have a temperature. You become concerned, however, because you don't know how serious it is and whether or not the condition will worsen. So you take them to the doctor. On examination, your doctor tells you, "Yes, it's the flu. There's a lot of this going around right now. Just provide lots of fluids and rest. You'll see improvement in a few days."

You go home feeling much more relaxed, even though nothing has really changed. The doctor has really done nothing to help you. So why do you feel better? Because you found out that their symptoms were normal, that other kids are going through the same thing, and that they will get over it, just given some time.

So it is with your children's reaction to divorce. I want to describe to you what the normal symptoms are, assure you that there are other kids going through the same thing, and reassure you that your children will reach a point of acceptance, even though it may take more time than you thought.

The amount of time that it takes for your children to recover from the trauma of your divorce, and the intensity of their reaction, may vary. But the emotional stages that they go through seem to be fairly consistent. Researchers have indicated that children's reaction to divorce approximates the same stages of grieving that adults experience when they lose a loved one through death or the breaking off of a significant relationship. This seems to be true across a wide range of ages, including adult children of divorce.

From preschoolers to adult children, there appears to be an instinctive process of grieving. Yet the way the stages of grieving are experienced, and the speed of the process, seem to be dependent on a number of factors. These include but are not limited to: the age of the children, the sex of the children, the way the children relate to both father and mother, the way Mom and Dad relate to each other, and the stability of the children's environment.

# THE INITIAL STAGE

For the sake of simplicity, I have divided the grieving process into three stages: initial, secondary, and acceptance. Within the initial stage, which is the topic of this chapter, there are several predominant emotions, which are typically handled by two basic reactions: denial and anger.

These two reactions, and the behaviors which go with them, are the first two stages of the grieving process. These are merely the children's way of handling their emotional crises. Most children will jump from stage to stage, regressing numerous times before reaching a point of acceptance. Even when acceptance is the predominant condition (usually two to five years after the marital disruption), children will relapse into grieving whenever new stresses enter their lives. These "residual" influences can extend well into their adult years, affecting their own marriages, as well as the way they raise their children.

The diagram on page 55 illustrates the way children deal with input during the initial stage. The arrows represent input from the environment, which is just a fancy way of saying "all the junk your child gets hit with on a daily basis." The outer circle is the defense system, which is a natural and instinctive protection of your inner self. The inner self is just an expression that I use to describe the essence of your personality, or your true self.

As indicated by the diagram, during the initial onslaught of information regarding the breakup of the family, your children protect themselves from this devastating news by deflecting the information. At first they use denial. But as shown in the illustration, as much as your children deny the truth, some information still seeps in, so that you are eventually forced to "face the music" (represented by the fading dotted lines). At that point, many children become very angry, and will use their anger to deflect what they can't deal with.

Sammy, at age five, did just that. When his dad

# Stage One: Initial Reactions

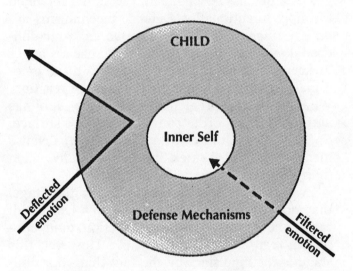

## Defense Mechanisms: Denial and Anger

first told him that he was going to be moving out, Sammy acted as if nothing had changed. His dad was elated that the dreaded news was so easily received. But as Sammy's dad unpacked items into his new apartment, he found red marker scribbled all over several of his dress shirts. When he confronted Sammy with the damage, Sammy threw a temper tantrum, kicking and screaming at his dad.

When I say that your children use denial or anger as a defense mechanism, this is not intended to imply intentionality. Defense mechanisms are largely unconscious. In other words, your children do not say, "Now I'm going to use my anger to keep from getting hurt." Rather, these emotional responses are like a blinking-eye reaction. When the eye is threatened by an object, it blinks automatically in order to protect the eye surface. So it is with children's (and our own) defense mechanisms. They kick in automatically when there is a threat of emotional hurt.

Even though someone is in the initial stage, that does not mean that they won't feel a full range of emotions, including rejection, guilt, confusion, fear, sadness, anxiety, etc. However, this stage is distinguished by the fact that your children will deal primarily with all of these feelings through denial and anger. Denial and anger take different forms in children of divorce within a variety of age groups.

# DENIAL

Denial corresponds with the initial realization, "My parents are getting a divorce!" For some

## THE INITIAL STAGE

children this is an insight or conclusion that they reach on their own due to overwhelming evidence of some problem within the family. For others, their first indication of trouble at home is when Mom or Dad sits them down and tells them the disturbing news. For most, however, it is a combination of evidence within the family and comments that have been made to them by both Mom and Dad.

Whatever the case, children are not prepared to handle the news that their whole world is about to come apart. This initial shock is met with comments or thoughts such as, "This can't be happening to me." Or, "I'm sure they will work everything out; I know my parents really love each other." As seen in the previous diagram, both of these comments serve to deflect the truth.

Denial is similar to actual physical shock. When people go into shock, they are literally able to numb the pain temporarily. They might even show a greater level of ability, as when an injured accident victim is able to rescue his entire family from a burning vehicle. It isn't until later that the pain becomes acute, and the person realizes the extent of the injuries.

So it is with children who first learn that their parents are about to separate or divorce. The mind goes into a type of emotional shock, which temporarily numbs the pain. I believe that this is a God–given, natural reaction, which we as parents should recognize and accept, and maybe even be thankful for. Denial of an emotional blow has its place in preparing the way for eventual acceptance.

# Preschoolers

As in the example of Bobby (from chapter 3), his mom was pleasantly surprised at how well her son seemed to take the news of his parents' divorce. This is particularly true of preschoolers (ages two to six), who are not at a developmental stage where they can understand the implications of their family breakup. Their concrete and magical thinking tell them, "Mom and Dad have had fights before. I'm sure they'll work this one out, too." Many times they work through their denial through fantasy play, in which they pretend that everything works out just fine, and that "we all live happily ever after."

Denial spares the preschooler unbearable pain. You see, to a preschooler, their whole world is their family. They have no sense of friends, or job, or church activities, as adults usually have. For them, their whole world is about to fall apart. How can we expect them to understand and accept?

Don't be surprised if your preschooler does not express any of these emotions. Typically, they cannot express what they are thinking or feeling because usually they don't even know themselves. You have to try to understand their feelings by watching their behavior and then trying to interpret what's going on inside their minds.

One interesting reaction was recently shared with me by the mother of a preschool boy. After telling her young son the devastating news of his father's imminent departure, her son responded with, "Can I go out and play now?"

The comment might be considered unusual, but the underlying reaction is typical. Many parents report that their children seem to go on as if nothing has changed. The only noticeable difference might be that the children are a little more possessive, especially whenever you want to go out without them.

## School–aged Children

For school–aged children (ages six to twelve) you can expect a similar type of denial. However, you might hear more questions about how their lives might change. At this age your children are just as stunned, but now they have better intellectual ability to reason and question.

In some cases, including some teenagers, your children's behavior might even improve during this time. One parent told me that her two children suddenly stopped bickering with one another. They started doing their chores without being told, and were generally very well behaved. "How do you explain that behavior?" she asked.

The explanation which I gave has to do with

this denial stage. As the children deny their own feelings, they may also recognize the fact that Mom or Dad is really hurting. So they "cool it" around the house for a while until "things blow over."

Unfortunately, this reaction doesn't last very long. As the denial wears off, the children become aware of their own hurts and begin to act out their own pain. Enjoy the good behavior while it lasts!

# Teenagers

For teenagers, denial can take the same forms as those already mentioned, but may also demonstrate itself through increased activity outside the home. This, by the way, is the method by which many adults handle their denial. They immerse themselves in work or a hobby, or just refuse to think about what is going on.

Typically, teenagers are seeking independence, no matter what the family dynamics are like. So when you add the news, "Mom and Dad are splitting up," then you'll see many teenagers begin to seek excuses to get out of the house. Whether it's a ballteam, a church youth group, or a new intense friendship, your teenagers may seem to vanish in order to avoid or block out the pain they may be trying to deny.

One mother of a sixteen–year–old boy recently

told me about her son's relationship with his girl-friend.

> My son had been dating this girl for about six months. Once I told him about his father and I breaking up, he seemed to lean on her completely. I'm glad he has her, but I'm concerned that he's over at her house *all* the time! He eats there, hangs out there, and seems to do everything but sleep there. He was never like that before his father left. Do you think it's because he's mad at me?

It is more likely that the boy is in the denial stage. Her son has merely intensified his relationship in order to take his mind off, or deflect, the problems he has to face at home. This can work for a while, but sooner or later her son will have to face the reality of his parents' breakup.

# Adults

For those who are considered to be adults (over eighteen), there is the expectation that they will not be affected as much by their parents' breakup. Research has not found this to be true. In the initial stage, adult children of divorce tend to react much like their younger counterparts. Their denial merely reflects their disbelief that this could be happening to them.

Many times this age group is away from home,

and is less dependent on Mom and Dad. Yet they still seem to go through the same denial that younger children experience. Their way of dealing with the denial is usually to immerse themselves in work, school projects, or other social relationships. Another common tactic is to pretend that the divorce will have no bearing on their lives.

One college student told me, "I'm on my own now. What happens to my parents at this point doesn't affect me. I'm more concerned for my little brother."

This same student later dropped out of school, partially due to grades, but also because things at home were "falling apart." Whatever the reason, the truth was that he *was* affected. This student had a lot to work through before he could go back to school.

Then there are the adults who are married and have families of their own. When they hear about a parental divorce they tend to react with the same disbelief. Many times they fall into the role of "parenting their parents," as do some younger adults and teens, trying to mediate the conflict. Although this may be a natural reaction, parents should not encourage their adult children's nurturing instincts since this is an unhealthy family pattern. Instead, adult children of divorce need to care for themselves and their own families. Divorcing parents should assure their children that they will seek the help they need from a more neutral and appropriate person.

For adults, denial does not last as long as in children. Since they possess higher order thought processes and abstract reasoning skills, they tend to become more quickly aware of what went wrong, who did what first, and why things are not going to work out. Their biggest dilemma is usually their loyalty conflicts, which remain the major issue throughout the rest of the grieving process.

# MOVING ON

Is this denial bad or wrong? Not at all! It's a normal, God–given reaction to devastating news. It's what keeps us from going crazy when news is too difficult to comprehend. Without denial we would be overwhelmed by anxiety. We all use it as a defense mechanism. Children in particular will use denial since they have no other way of controlling adults or their actions.

How can I help my children move beyond their denial? The truth of the matter is that there is very little you can do. And perhaps you shouldn't even try, since this is a natural defense for working through pain. Give your children time to adjust their thinking, and let denial run its natural course. Try not to increase their anxiety by reacting in extreme ways.

Children, particularly the younger ones, are not sophisticated enough to figure out that by staying in denial they can avoid some of the bad feelings they have about the divorce. Actually, we adults (and some teenagers) are more often guilty on that count. So it's not that they are using denial on purpose. They will move on in their healing when they are emotionally ready to deal with it. Creating a stable environment as quickly as possible will help children pass through this stage more easily.

Parents can help their kids deal with reality by giving them clear, honest answers to all their questions. Trying to gloss over the truth to save their feelings will only help them to avoid reality for a little longer, which needlessly extends the healing process.

A common example of how you can help your children face reality is how you face every holiday season. Think about that dreaded first Christmas as a separated couple. Parents often explain to me how one spouse is going to come over Christmas Eve or Christmas morning so that they can spend Christmas Day together just as they always have. Even though this noble effort seems to be in keeping with the spirit of peace and good cheer, I'm afraid it only increases the anxiety and feeds the denial of our children (and many times the parents).

In a way you are acting out a lie, without actually lying. Acting happy and "together" helps your children hold on to the fantasy that "our family will be fine." Remember, the more quickly you begin to build new traditions, such as: "We go to Dad's on Christmas Eve and spend Christmas

## THE INITIAL STAGE

Day with Mom," the sooner you and your kids will be able to move on with your lives—and heal.

Giving your children honest information, and not playacting in front of them, will help them realize that the separation and imminent divorce of their parents are realities they will have to face. As they do, two of the first feelings that come rushing in are insecurity and fear. This should not surprise us. It's incredibly unsettling to find out that your whole world is falling apart.

Such is true even for those eager and sometimes overly confident teenagers. They want to go out and discover a whole new life for themselves —one that is completely independent of their parents. But what they don't tell you, and they may not realize themselves, is that they also want to come home to a safe environment. They become painfully aware of this need once that familiar homelife is taken away from them. They become angry because, after all, "It's not fair!" For teenagers, "fairness" is judged in relation to their own needs.

As we have seen in the diagram on page 55, even though we deny, some realizations inevitably trickle into our inner selves (as demonstrated by the dotted lines). Once these realizations accumulate to a point where we must face certain issues, we are filled with fear and anxiety. The way most children of divorce handle their fears and anxieties during the initial stage is with anger. This is considered by many to be the second stage of grieving, and is another way we all deflect painful information that we may not be ready to deal with. Anger is just another tool that we and our children use to protect ourselves from the reality of the situation.

# ANGER

As time goes on, and more of the reality filters through your children's defense mechanisms, they begin to recognize that they cannot make the problem go away through denial. Their fear leads them to the natural reaction of anger. Once again, as seen in the diagram, all they are doing is deflecting the pain of the situation. Sometimes it is deflected toward a person, while other times it is deflected toward the situation in general. In either case, children avoid dealing with reality by blaming others. The "Oh no, not me!" of denial, evolves into the "Why me?" of anger.

One boy said, "It's like when you first hear about it, you can't believe it's true! Then when you realize that it might actually happen, you get mad at your mom or dad or both. You think, "How can they do this to me? It's not fair!"

This is probably one of the most recognizable and familiar stages. Whenever people think about children of divorce, one of the stereotypes that comes to mind is the child who is the terror of the class or neighborhood—the Eddie Hysers of this world. Even though this stereotype is overstated, it is certainly true that children of divorce typically carry around unresolved anger. The ways in which they deal with their anger depend a lot on their personality, their sex, and their age.

## Sex Differences

In terms of sex differences, it is generally accepted that boys feel and demonstrate anger more openly than girls. This is not always true. Certainly personality differences can alter this generalization, but across most age groups, one can expect boys to react more angrily than their female counterparts. And even though they may get beyond the anger stage as their predominant reaction, they continue to show signs of anger throughout all of their stages of grieving, sometimes lasting a lifetime. This does not mean that girls do not get angry. Some show more anger than boys. But for the most part, girls are better able to express their feelings, and may be more adept at resolving their angry emotions. Perhaps because our culture has taught girls how to internalize their anger, we see less evidence of an angry reaction.

One possible exception, to this rule of thumb that boys react more strongly than girls, is found in several studies about adult children of divorce. When parents divorce with adult children in the house or out on their own, it is usually the girls who have more severe reactions. Their anger may be more internalized, but nonetheless they seem to bear the brunt of the dissolving family.

Two possibilities as to why this occurs are: 1) boys tend to move out and more quickly distance themselves emotionally, and 2) girls tend to be more nurturing, and place more value on family relationships. Therefore, when things begin to fall apart, they feel more compelled to get involved, and they may feel more upset about their inability to change the situation.

# Age Differences

Age differences are a bit more complicated than sex differences, due to the diversity of developmental changes, as outlined in chapter 2. For younger children (under twelve), their anger is often misplaced. This means they don't always direct their anger toward an appropriate target.

These angry feelings are typically expressed toward one or both parents, but can also be directed toward siblings, toward the future stepparent, and many times toward self. The younger the children are, the more likely they are to blame whoever happens to be around. This means that even though they might be angry at Dad for leaving, they will take their angry feelings out on the custodial parent (Mom).

For the reasons outlined in chapter 2, children under six years of age will blame themselves for their parents' breakup, and will feel anger toward self, or guilt. The younger the children, the more prevalent the guilty feelings are likely to be. These children believe that all of the family's activities revolve around them, and they can't help but feel like they must have done something wrong. This reaction can be a particular source of concern to parents, since it can lead to depression, self–condemnation, and, in the worst case, self–destructive behaviors.

Guilt can be a predominant feeling for other age groups during the angry stage, but as your children get older they are better able to understand your explanations that they had nothing to do with Dad's decision to leave. In fact, research has demonstrated that among children of divorce who are 18 or older, the feelings of guilt over the parental breakup are almost nonexistent.

## Young Children

How is anger displayed? For the youngest of the children, aggressive play and temper tantrums are increased, particularly when the custodial parent wants to go somewhere without them. Or anger may be most evident right before or after visitation with the noncustodial parent.

One parent recently told me about her "well–behaved" daughter who would turn into a terror every other weekend, about the time of her father's visitation. The mother asked me whether or not this was good enough reason to try to cut off visitation rights, since the child was obviously re-acting angrily to the thought of her father's visit.

I responded with the fact that this is a fairly typical reaction to the insecurity and anxiety the girl feels about the changing of households. This reaction will subside as the child works through the angry stage and becomes more accustomed to the fact that she visits with Dad every other week-end. There may be absolutely nothing scary about visiting with Dad. And usually the child is fine once she gets there.

Yet many children have strong angry reactions just before the visit is to commence. I conclude that this is more a reflection of the anger they feel about the situation than anger toward a person. This does not mean that there are not times that you might need to look into what's going on while your kids are at the other parent's house. Don't jump to premature conclusions just because your children are resistant about going. It's probably best to seek a professional counselor's advice if visitations continue to be a problem for you and your kids.

Small children are also not as sophisticated at distinguishing who is to blame for the breakup. This may be particularly frustrating to the parent who wants to be sure the children know how in-nocent he or she was in the marital mess. Chil-dren will tend to blame the one who leaves, since their loyalty will be toward the one who sticks with them, no matter what the circumstances dic-tate. Contrasting this point is the fact that even though they may blame the parent who left, they are more likely to vent their anger on the parent who is present. This is not only because of availability, but also because they feel more free to show their anger to the parent with whom they feel most secure.

This has been a common complaint I've heard from many a discouraged single parent. One mom recently stated, "I can't understand how my child can stand there and shout, 'I hate you, Mommy!' I'm the one who does everything for her while her father does nothing!"

Try not to be overly hurt or upset by your children's anger. Remember, they are probably venting their feelings about the situation, or may even be using you as a sounding board because they trust that you won't leave them like their other parent did. One child put it this way: "You've already seen your dad leave, and even though you're mad at him, you want to make sure he'll come back again next weekend. So you take it out on your mom because you kind of know she'll always be there for you."

This by no means dictates that you, as the custodial parent, have to put up with abuse from your children. Try to understand their hurt, and try not to overreact out of your own frustration over the situation. But feel free to discipline children who are behaving disrespectfully or who are verbally abusive. They may be testing you to see if you care enough about them to discipline them. Remember, your children may try almost anything to get your attention, even if the attention is negative. Better to get Mom's attention through acting out than not to get her attention at all.

## Teenagers and Adults

For teenagers, displays of anger are certainly not foreign. In fact, many parents express the following dilemma: "I can't figure out how much of my teenager's anger is due to our divorce, and how much is just typical teenage rebellion." Nevertheless, when divorce occurs, many teens show increased signs of anger, resentment, and rebellion.

Unlike their younger siblings, teenagers will try to assess blame, and then may target their anger toward a particular person. This is why you may see teenagers refuse to visit or even speak to one of their parents. If the target of their anger happens to be the custodial parent (usually Mom), then rebellion and sabotage within the home can become so unbearable that Mom may give up and allow her teen to "run free," or just send the teenager to live with Dad.

When the lines of blame are not so distinct, which is much of the time, the teenagers' anger may be more generalized. This can be evident in their attitude and behavior toward parents and siblings, teachers and school, the church and God, and at times, their friends and themselves.

Teenage boys tend to be more aggressive with

their anger, while both boys and girls can demonstrate their anger through more passive means
(passive aggression). This can be seen in many
teens through their lack of cooperation, moodi-
ness, and ability to create turmoil for those
around them. A good example of passive/aggres-
sive thinking was expressed by one teen, who
said, "I don't get mad; I just get even!"

Ginny was just such a teen. She was fourteen
when her father moved out. Within a matter of
months, what was once a fairly compliant child
was now growing more and more resistant. She
started by talking back to both parents. This car-
ried over to some rudeness at school, which
prompted a phone call from the school counselor.
Next to be affected was her attendance at church.
She began to resist getting up on Sundays, which
soon became a refusal to go. Her involvement
within the church youth group faded, and was replaced with a new set of friends who were described as "questionable" by her mother. All of
these changes only seemed to alienate Ginny
from family and former friends.

In counseling, Ginny revealed a great deal of
anger. Yet the target of that anger did not seem to
stay focused. Her generalized anger meant that
she blamed everyone else for her confusion and
growing isolation. This became almost self–destructive, as Ginny was now only associating with
those who would lead her into more trouble. Indirectly, Ginny felt like she was getting back at
those who had wronged her, but in fact she was

mostly hurting herself. The child who is trying to "get even" can never "get ahead."

"It's not fair!" is a common theme of the teenager who is angry about their parents' divorce. In many ways they are right. It isn't fair. Anger is just a natural reaction to this injustice. The real question is: "How will your children display their anger?" As a parent, you cannot keep your children from experiencing this anguish, but you can try to help them work through their anger. Acknowledge that their sense of fairness *has* been violated, but explain that life isn't always fair. Hopefully, this experience will become an object lesson that children will use throughout their lives.

Guilty feelings during this stage are much less likely for teenagers than for those who are younger. They are usually too busy blaming everyone else for their problems to feel guilt about something they might have done. In a few cases, however, teenage children of divorce may feel guilt over their parents' breakup, particularly in situations where they have been the focus of difficulties or arguments in the home.

For adult children of divorce, there is little evidence that they feel any guilt at all. But there may be an increased feeling, particularly among women, of responsibility to help. They may try to get involved, and are much more likely to feel anger toward the active agent (the one who is seeking the divorce). Depending on the maturity of the individual, the anger of an adult is usually better managed than with teens or younger kids. Adult children are able to articulate their concerns, and have a better chance at resolving their angry feelings. If they don't live at home, they don't have to deal with the constant tension, and are more likely to have a satisfactory relationship with both parents.

# HELPING YOUR CHILDREN

How can I help my children work through their anger or guilt? Acknowledge your children's anger. If it's appropriate, affirm their right to be angry. This allows for more of the reality of the situation to actually filter into your children's life (as illustrated in the diagram on page 55). This can be very healthy.

Encourage free expression of their feelings. If you suspect that they may be blaming themselves, make sure you reassure them that the decision to end the marriage is strictly yours (and your spouse's), and has nothing to do with their behavior or actions. If your children are young, they may not understand this the first time you tell them, so continue to reassure them periodically just to make sure.

If you are the target of their angry feelings, try not to be defensive. It is most important that you are able to listen during this crucial time. It would be quite natural for you to defend yourself, or even to shout back at your children. But remember, your children are reacting out of feelings of fear and insecurity. They need to be sure that they are loved. Their behavior might even be an unconscious test to see if you will still love them even when they are bad. By listening, you reassure your children that you will not abandon them.

What if it is the absent parent who is the target of your children's anger? Once again, you must sit by and listen. *Do not join in and bad-mouth your ex!* As much as you might agree, or think your children would appreciate your reinforcement of their ideas, it's important that you resist this temptation. Your children might appreciate it for the time being, but in the long run it will only hurt your children's emotional growth and put them into a position of defending the other parent. It is much like the adage: *"I* can criticize my family, but *you* had better not try it."

Michael's mother found herself in this dilemma. She reported, "Whenever Michael gets back from visiting with his father he seems extremely agitated. He complains about everything. You'd think he hated going to his father's. But when I agree with him and suggest he just not go anymore, he immediately starts telling me all the wonderful things that he likes about his father. He sure has me confused."

There are some times when helping your children deal with their anger requires you to go beyond just listening to them or helping them to express their feelings. You must patiently endure temper tantrums, long silences when they refuse to speak, and other belligerent behaviors.

As difficult as it might be, try to ignore minor infractions and outbursts. And when needed, don't be afraid to discipline your children lovingly. (See the appendix on discipline.) But above all, try not to be drawn into a fight. To respond in kind will only increase your children's anger and make you feel as immature as your children are acting. Please note, however, that you will fail from time to time. This is inevitable. After all, you are going through your own struggles. When you do mess up, tell your children you were wrong and then start over again, trying to model an appropriate way of dealing with anger.

In the worst of situations, your children's anger will lead them into behaviors that you cannot afford to ignore. Unfortunately, teens in particular have many dangerous options available to them at a time when they might not be thinking clearly. Drugs and alcohol are the most obvious examples of this, but other areas include school truancy, promiscuous sex, and even criminal activity. If you suspect your children of participating in any such activities, seek professional help as soon as possible. You must take this type of behavior very seriously, and try to nip it in the bud. By quickly treating the symptoms, you have a better chance of keeping the problem from getting worse, and you have a greater opportunity to get to the heart of the problem before your children become unreachable.

Professional help can come in the form of a counselor or psychologist, especially if you know of one who specializes in treating children of divorce. If you are not familiar with anyone like this, check with your family physician, the school psychologist, or a pastor who knows your situation and can make an educated referral.

# MOVING ON

Eventually, as with denial, enough truth filters through the defense barriers so that our children once again get a glimpse of reality. They realize, unconsciously, that their denial did not work, and that their anger only brought them more pain. Gradually they are able to process what is going on in their lives and what is happening to their family. And even though they are distorting the reality around them, they are now able to deal with it at some level. This is what indicates that they are moving on to the secondary stage.

Denial and anger are presented here not as an exclusive list of the reactions your children will have when first confronted with separation or divorce. Certainly there are many emotions and many reactions. In addition, even though these stages are presented in an orderly, sequential fashion, your children may jump from one stage to another—over and over again. In other words, even though your children move well beyond the initial stage, don't be surprised to see them regress to some form of initial reaction whenever a new family trauma or change occurs. These regressions are occasionally evident during holidays or anniversary dates of the breakup, or whenever your children are reminded of the depth of their loss.

How long does this initial stage last? The speed at which your children move through the stages of grieving is an individual process. This depends on their personality, as well as how easily your divorce unfolds. I know that there is no such thing as an easy divorce, but it does help your recovery and the recovery of your children, when you and your ex can work together for an amicable separation and divorce. This will be discussed further in a later chapter.

In any case, you have to expect that it will take several months for your children to work through this initial period. It is not unusual for some children to take a year or more to work through their denial and anger. If you find that they seem to be stuck in one of these stages, you may want to seek professional advice. It is also noteworthy that some children experience delayed reactions, as discussed in chapter 2. This delay can be a form of denial in which your children seem to have no reaction at all until a year or more later. Then they begin the grieving process. This is most likely in the case of very young children (five and under) who do not understand what has happened, or how it will affect their lives. As they grow and develop, they may start their grieving process one or more years later.

## CHAPTER SUMMARY

In this chapter, we have examined your children's initial reactions to the news that a separation or divorce is about to occur. They are immediately flooded with a myriad of emotions, but generally react in two basic stages. The first is denial, which is the result of the children's inability to cope with the devastating news of the family breakup. Once your children gain a glimpse of the reality of their situation, they are filled with fears and insecurities about their lives and future. This fear pushes your children into the next stage, which is anger—anger about the situation or toward one or both parents.

These initial emotions can last anywhere from a few weeks to a few years, but a more normal time frame would be two to ten months. Helping your children move along in the healing process involves your giving them honest, clear information, and encouraging open expression of their emotions. As the truth filters through their defensive exteriors, your children will be able to move on to the next stage of the grieving process. Additional guidelines on helping your children move along in the emotional stages will be presented in the third section of this book.

# THE SECONDARY STAGE

I know when my dad first left I was really mad at him. I blamed him for all the problems in the house, especially when I would see my mom crying. That would make me want to go over to his place and punch him out. But when I was with my dad, I never said a word about how I was feeling. I was afraid he would leave for good. Then, as I started to accept the fact that my parents were getting a divorce, I think I just gave up. I gave up on school, the track team—just about everything. I didn't feel like doing things anymore. I spent most of my time just sitting in my room, listening to tapes.

—a fourteen–year–old boy

Beyond the initial denial and anger stage, children usually become very frustrated, because they learn that they can't make problems disappear by pretending they're not there, and because their anger only seems to make problems worse. These realizations lead your children to begin feeling even worse than they did before. They are unable to protect themselves from all of the negative things going on around them, or from the onslaught of feelings they are experiencing.

In terms of the diagram on page 55, even though your children have been able to deflect many incoming arrows, some painful realizations have managed to filter in and affect their inner selves (represented by the dotted lines).

In addition, as time passes, your children become emotionally stronger and are better able to face the pain. Their defense mechanisms ease a bit, since they are now better able to handle the reality of the situation. With more and more of the truth affecting your children, soon they can no longer use deflection to protect themselves. This change marks the beginning of the secondary stage.

This new stage is distinguished by the fact your children's primary way of dealing with their situation has changed from deflection to distortion and filtering of information. Look at the following diagram. Now, the arrows of input are able to reach the inner self, which means they begin to affect the children, perhaps even causing your children to feel worse. You will notice, however, that the input is distorted or faded by remaining defenses. These new defense mechanisms are necessary. Even though the children are stronger,

# Stage Two: Secondary Reactions

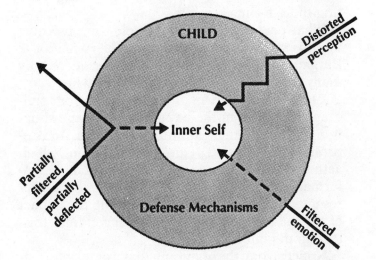

## Defense Mechanisms: Bargaining and Depression

they are still unable to deal honestly or fully with their changing world.

Your children's feelings during the secondary stage may be similar to what they felt during the initial stage: rejection, anger, confusion, sadness, guilt, frustration, and depression. But now they are handling the feelings differently. Instead of denying their feelings, or deflecting them by blaming others, they are now allowing themselves to feel. They are still too fragile to experience emotion fully. But they *are* able to begin letting these feelings sink in.

What new methods do your children use during this stage in order to handle their emotions? Bargaining and depression are considered by many to be the next two stages of grieving.

Bargaining is a form of manipulation your children use to lessen the pain, or change the situation in order to make it more acceptable. And depression is a natural emotional reaction, which actually deadens the pain or distorts incoming information. In the diagram on page 83, this is represented by the dotted lines (lessening the impact of the information), and the zigzagged lines (distorting the information).

Notice from the diagram that some information is still deflected. This indicates that even though your children have moved on to the secondary stage, sometimes information is still too hard to deal with, or the children regress to the point that they once again deny or react in anger.

The paradox in this stage is that even though your children are emotionally stronger, they are probably experiencing more pain. This is just part of the grieving process. In many ways, your children must hurt more before they can begin to get better. This is called "bottoming out." We will see this more clearly as we discuss both bargaining and depression in more detail.

# BARGAINING

Even though the bargaining stage is presented here as the third way your children may try to deal with their emotions, this defense mechanism may be observed throughout the secondary stage. It is probably one of the most difficult stages to understand and recognize. Simply put, it is when your children become so frustrated with the situation that they try to find simple solutions to a very complex problem. The complex problem is the fact that their parents are getting a divorce. The simple solutions are the children's feeble attempts to manipulate their parents' actions toward a desired outcome.

# YOUNGER CHILDREN

For young children the motivation behind bargaining is frustration. Your children merely want to make the pain go away, and many times the goal is "to get my parents back together." For younger children this usually involves fantasy and magical thinking. But for those who are eight or older, actual manipulation of the situation is apparent.

It is hard to recognize the bargaining stage, because there is some form of bargaining throughout all of the stages. In fact, as I describe its symptoms, many of you will think, "My kids do that all the time." What distinguishes this as an actual stage is the fact that your children will use bargaining as their predominant defense mechanism. This usually results from frustration. Children might believe that the only way they're going to feel better is to get their parents back together. Another possible solution to their anger, guilt, or sadness is to see if they can help their parent find a new spouse.

If these solutions don't sound familiar to you, that's because your children do not verbalize these ideas; they only *think* them. Since your younger children are not sophisticated enough to figure out how to make their wishes come true, they only fantasize to each other about their parents getting remarried. Sometimes they will unconsciously act on those fantasies.

Ryan is a good example of this phenomenon. Ryan's mom and dad had been divorced for about three months. He had been showing signs of anger toward Mom and toward authority figures at school, but was now finally settling down to more normal behavior. It was at this time that Mom began to date a man she met at night school. Those of you who are single parents can predict what happened next. Whenever Mom's new friend came over to visit or to pick her up for a date, Ryan behaved at his all-time worst.

Ryan, who is only seven, probably did not think, "Let's see how I can sabotage this relationship." In fact, while talking with me, he said he liked his mother's boyfriend. But what he didn't say, and did not even realize, was that this new man in his mom's life was a threat to his ongoing fantasy that someday Mom and Dad would get back together.

Another common example can be found in Tracy, who at age four knew that if she pushed her mom to the limit right around bedtime, Mom would call Dad to come over and discipline his daughter. Of course, as soon as Dad arrived, Tracy would go right to bed with barely a whimper, which only encouraged Mom to call Dad the next time it happened. This went on a number of times until Tracy's parents realized that the motivation behind the misbehavior was to get Mom and Dad back together, at least for the evening.

## Teenagers and Adults

For older children, especially teenagers, attempts at manipulating the situation are usually more overt. They may verbalize their desires, and then work behind the scenes when you don't comply with their wishes. I have heard of many examples from children of divorce who talk about how they relay (or mis-relay) messages between their parents. They change the tone or content of the message in order to accomplish some purpose, usually trying to draw parents together, or drive them farther apart. I find it incredible to see how often this works, and how long kids can get away with this type of bargaining. It seems to work best when parents do not speak, but use their kids to communicate to each other—literally putting them in the middle.

Other teens, who are less devious perhaps, will not give misinformation, but will give just enough detail, or omit just enough, to convey the message they want heard. One fourteen–year–old girl did this as she told Mom how hurt Dad seemed, how bleak his apartment looked, and how lonely he appeared. Perhaps if Mom felt sorry for him, she would not be as mad.

For adult children of divorce, bargaining usually involves their getting into the middle of things—if not to mediate and get parents back together, then to comfort one or both parents through their suffering. This difficult role takes its toll on children. The effects of your divorce can sometimes be just as devastating to your adult children as they are to you. That is why they try to do whatever they can to help make the pain go away—just as you do.

# Helping Your Children

The best way to thwart this type of activity is for parents not to allow their children to be caught in the middle. Negotiate with your ex, person to person. If you did not get your support check for the month, don't ask the kids to "just mention it to your father when you see him." The better you are at co-parenting, the more likely it will be that you will have open communication with your ex. And then your children will be less likely to believe that they can change their home circumstances through any form of bargaining.

Bargaining is a lot like denial in that the motivation behind both is to help make the pain go away. For both stages your part is to help your children deal with the reality they will have to face. It seems cruel to say that you shouldn't sugarcoat the situation in order to save your children some pain. But the truth is that the sooner your children learn the truth, the more quickly they can begin to deal with it and move forward in their lives.

One final note about the frustration and bargaining that children experience. These feelings may not present themselves as a separate stage. Instead, they may be intermingled with other stages, including denial, anger, guilt, and the next stage to be discussed, depression.

# DEPRESSION

Thus far, we have described all of your children's emotional reactions as defense mechanisms. Yet it is hard to imagine depression as a defense against anything. Actually, depression is a natural reaction to overwhelming life change and pain. It's like an electrical switchboard, which shuts down when it is overloaded with current. This crisis situation may inconvenience a lot of people, but without such safeguards, there may have been a fire or explosion.

Such depression is referred to as reactive depression, since it occurs in reaction to specific life stresses. This is different from depression caused by chemical imbalance, hormonal change, or hereditary predisposition. These latter depressions need to be treated by a qualified professional. Contact your family doctor for a referral if such a depression is apparent. Assuming your children's depression is merely reactive, you need to understand that this is a natural and necessary part of your children's grieving. It is also the way your children protect themselves from more extensive damage. So, in this sense, depression is a defense mechanism.

Most of us are familiar with the depression and anxiety described in this stage because at some time in our lives we experienced it firsthand. However, many of us may be surprised to learn that children get depressed and overly anxious, too. I have talked with four- and five-year-olds who have mentioned suicide as an escape from their problems.

Depression usually begins once the reality of the situation sets in. The children have moved beyond denial and recognize that they cannot control their parents or the situation. Their anger and guilt have only made them feel worse, so they give up. They have learned that they are totally helpless to change the situation, and must accept the way things are. That's depressing!

Being in the depression stage does not mean that your children will not slip back into anger or bargaining. In fact, it is common for children to slide back and forth between all of the stages like an emotional roller coaster, sometimes on a daily basis.

Most of us know how we feel when we're depressed or anxious. But how can you recognize it in your children, especially when they are too young, or are unable to express how they feel? Childhood depression is different from adult depression because it can be so varied. Children can show depression through sadness, increased anxiety, distractibility, resentment, sullenness, regression, confusion, lack of interest in social activities, loss of appetite, and even through acting out behaviors. The way your children demonstrate their depression will depend on their age and personality.

# Younger Children

For younger children, (eight or under) depression can appear as sadness and withdrawal, while others (especially boys) may actually show signs of increased activity and acting out. This has been called masked depression, because it seems almost opposite of what we regard as typical depression. Even though these children seem to have a high activity level and to be quite anxious, the underlying feeling is still depression. They merely cover their sadness with tasks or trouble-making.

If your children are in school, you can expect to see lowered school performance due to increased distractibility and regression. This regression is an interesting phenomenon where children seem to go backward developmentally. Toilet–trained preschoolers will start having accidents again; others will regress to baby talk; skills that were once known will seem to be forgotten.

I remember one incident while I was consulting in an elementary school. A teacher came to me and said that she thought one of her first–grade students had a brain tumor. I asked her why she thought that. She replied, "Brian started the school year knowing how to write his name and all the letters of the alphabet. As the year progressed, he began to make mistakes on his last name, then didn't know how to write several letters, and now only seems to be able to write a few letters. Is it possible for a child to forget that much in just a few months?" My immediate response was, "What's going on at home?"

As we looked into the situation, we found out that the father had left home about two weeks into the school year. Since then there had been a lot of discord in the home.

Regression seems logical when you view the sense of loss from the children's perspective. As they move along, growing in knowledge and independence, suddenly their whole world seems to start falling apart. They immediately go back to an earlier, more comfortable stage of development. This helps them feel more secure. They stay there until they feel comfortable enough to step out again in new directions. As adults, don't we do the same thing? We find ourselves retreating to our parents' house, or taking an easier job, or acting more like a teenager than an adult.

In addition to regression, some preschoolers and young children will demonstrate their depression through insecurity and possessive dependence. Your children may seem overly anxious, complain of stomachaches, lose their appetite, lose sleep, or develop school phobia. School phobia, and the way they cling to you whenever you try to go out, are really just symptoms of the insecurity and anxiety they feel. "Will Mom leave me, too?" "I wonder if Dad will come back." "How will we pay our bills?" "Will we have to move, or will I have to go to a different school?" "Why didn't God stop this from happening to us?" These, and a hundred other questions like them, all enter your children's mind, with no apparent answers.

For young children there is little for them to do but wait for the situation to become more stable and secure. This will take time—time for them to grow up, and time for them to see that they can begin to trust again. As a parent, you want to provide an environment that will speed this healing process.

# Teenagers and Adults

For teenagers and young adults, depression is more recognizable because it is similar to the feelings of adults. As your children mature, they gain ability to express the way they are feeling. This assumes, however, that they are willing to talk to you. Usually, one of the byproducts of depression is the feeling that no one understands and no one cares. This alienation is particularly strong in teenagers. Divorce acts as a catalyst for more extreme rebellious reactions.

Other symptoms of depression include: eating and sleeping disturbances, low self–image, expressions of worthlessness and hopelessness, regression to a more immature stage, lowered school performance along with heightened distractibility, social and peer difficulties, lack of interest in activities that were once of interest, and, in the worst cases, escaping reality through drug and alcohol abuse.

Fortunately, these symptoms are the exception rather than the rule. Most preteens and teenagers seem to go on as usual, yet they have a sense of loss or sadness which is only noticeable to those who are closest to them. As a parent you may sense their increased isolation and sadness. It may seem more like preoccupation and/or emotional distance.

This was the case for Jenny. She showed a very slight reaction throughout her parents' separa-

## THE SECONDARY STAGE

tion and divorce. She didn't even react when her father remarried just a few months after her parents' divorce. Her mother thought Jenny was doing well, but referred her to me when she noticed that her daughter was losing interest in many of her former hobbies, and her school reported her to be falling behind in her work.

When Jenny first came in, she appeared to be a very mature fourteen–year–old young woman. She talked about how well she was doing with all of the changes in her life, as if she were trying to convince me that she didn't need to be there. As we talked, over a period of weeks, she began to talk about her loss.

> I was always considered to be Daddy's girl. I had no idea that he had a whole other life with some other family. Now he's married to Pam, who has her own two children. He comes around here to see me every other weekend. But what hurts the most is knowing that he is spending every night with Pam's kids. I'm sure he'll start loving them more and more until he forgets all about me. My life will never be the same!

You can probably see how Jenny's sense of loss is similar to that of her mom. Jenny feels like she has been betrayed and replaced. Yet when I asked Jenny why she had never talked to her mom about any of this, she said, "My mom feels bad enough. She cries a lot and I know she feels like she's been rejected. I need to be strong so that at least she won't worry about how I'm doing."

Boys tend to have more severe depression. During this stage junior high and senior high boys can go through a year or more of distractibility, problems in school, social difficulties, and passive aggression. Just as with masked depression in younger kids, older students can underhandedly try to get back at others as part of their depression.

Matthew, at age fifteen, was demonstrating this type of depression. He had gone through the denial and anger stages. Now, about a year later, he was beginning to settle down and let the reality of the situation sink in. As things at home were being resolved, Mom was beginning to think that the problems were over. She was surprised when she got a call from the school asking her to come in for a parent/teacher conference.

It seems Matthew had not been bringing in his homework assignments, including several large projects. In addition, he had been cited for being late to several classes, and had two unexcused absences. Needless to say, Matthew's mother was shocked at this revelation.

When she confronted Matthew with his behaviors, he merely shrugged his shoulders and grunted. Over a period of weeks, the situation showed no improvement, so his mother brought him in for counseling.

At first, Matthew was an unwilling participant in the counseling sessions. But as rapport was built, he began to share his apathy toward life and toward his schoolwork. According to Matthew:

> My parents obviously don't care about me. My dad's gone, and my mom is always either at work or out with her friends. My needs and concerns are not important to anyone, so why should I care about my schoolwork? Besides, the only time my parents talk to me is when I screw up. So this time I really screwed up! You should hear them screaming now.

It doesn't take a psychologist to figure out that Matthew is depressed and seeking attention. However, he is also mad at his parents and believes that he is indirectly getting back at them by doing poorly in school. He needs to learn how to express his feelings appropriately, and then recognize that his performance at school is only hurting himself. We spent the next five weeks trying to get him to understand that concept.

For adult children of divorce it is sometimes surprising how depressing divorce can be. Many parents think that because the kids are older, and maybe even out of the house, they won't be as affected. But, having talked with dozens of adult children, I know that their parents' divorce can literally send them into a tailspin. They have reported loss of appetite, loss of sleep, inability to focus attention, excessive daydreaming, lack of ambition, and a feeling of numbness. When adult children are still in the home, they sometimes end up feeding their parents' pain by discussing events over and over. One woman reported it this way, "We had a house full of depressed people, mirroring each other's anguish and suffering. This went on for months, until one of my sisters started coming out of it. As she got help for herself, she gave the rest of us the courage to begin looking forward."

# HELPING YOUR CHILD

In time, your children, whatever their age, really do "bottom out." They reach a point at which they give up. They stop trying to get Mom and Dad back together; they stop believing that life can go on without adjustments; they come to the point where they are ready to face the truth, no matter how hurtful it might be. Once they begin to deal honestly with their situation, they are on their way to a point of acceptance.

Even though the depression stage can be one of the longest and most uncomfortable stages, it does serve several useful purposes. Let me list a few.

- Since people usually shut down during times of depression, this stage tends to provide your children with more peace of mind than previous stages. This reaction

varies, depending on your children's personality.

- They probably stop trying to control the situation, and begin to accept things as they are.
- For the first time, they are beginning to deal honestly with themselves about the divorce, and are taking a serious look at how it will affect their lives.
- Depression usually signals the fact that your children are at or near the bottom of the grieving process, and are bound to start looking up soon.

It is important to remember that this stage is a normal and necessary part of the grieving process. As parents, we should not negate or rush our children's emotions. Don't say to your children, "Stop moping around. Your father's gone, and the sooner you get used to the idea, the better." Give them the time that they need to grieve. Don't add to their pain by reminding them about all they have lost. But don't force them to pretend that all is well, when they still hurt inside.

Here are a few other suggestions for helping your children through their depression:

- Encourage them to talk to you about their feelings. Make sure you always acknowledge the depth of their loss.
- Don't be afraid to grieve in front of them, but don't model hopelessness or hysteria. They need to learn from you that it is okay

to cry, but they don't need to see you out of control.

- Help your children accept the reality of the situation by telling them the truth. Don't hold out false hope in order to keep them from being hurt. It's better to answer their questions honestly so that they can begin the healing process. Honesty will also help them as they try to rebuild new trust in you.
- Try to find some healthy activities for your children to get involved in. These could include a hobby, church activity, or school function—anything which might help your children focus on something positive.

If depression persists, consult an appropriate professional. And if despair or emotional mood swings seem severe, such as suicidal thoughts, seek immediate help.

# HOW LONG WILL THIS GO ON?

The secondary stage can take as much as a year to work through. And the entire grieving process can take two or more years. There are wide individual differences in the amount of time it takes your children to reach acceptance. These are considered to be the short–term effects of divorce on children. The long–term effects are thought to be those that occur after children reach a point of acceptance, usually two to five years after the actual divorce. These effects will be discussed in chapter 7.

Why does the healing process take so long? Rather than a slow, steady progression of emotional growth, the healing process can probably best be described as two steps forward, one step back. As your children move toward acceptance, maybe even reaching that point at times, inevitably something happens to send them right back down that emotional roller coaster, which we call the "slippery slope." That is why your children will need at least two full years to pass before they become confident in their acceptance.

They need to experience at least two Christmases, two Easters, and two birthdays in their new family before they can feel comfortable with their new living arrangement. And this assumes that the transition has gone fairly smoothly. If you add a new marriage by one of the parents, or a relocation, or any significant family change, then you can see how their recovery can take a much longer period of time.

## CHAPTER SUMMARY

In this chapter, we have examined the secondary stage in your children's recovery from divorce. We have seen how your children move from denial and anger, through bargaining and depression, and eventually approach a point of acceptance. During this process, we have seen how children will feel worse, even though they are progressing. This paradox continues until the children eventually "bottom out." Barring any new disruptions, this is followed by a period of gradual movement toward acceptance.

In addition, we have discussed how you can help your children move along in their recovery without pushing them before they are ready. As parents, you need to expect that this grieving process will take at least two years to complete, and that any significant family trauma or change will lengthen the recovery. Providing your children with a warm and stable home environment, along with a consistent, stress-free visitation arrangement, are the best ways to help your children reach a point of acceptance.

# THE ACCEPTANCE STAGE

As bad as my parents' divorce was, I know it has made me the person I am today. I think I've gained a different way of looking at the world. It has forced me to take a more realistic view. I realize now that life doesn't have to be fair! I know that things will not always go the way I want them to. Moving on with my life has to be a process of accepting what has happened, and trying to make the most of it. In school, I don't see too many kids with that kind of attitude. I figure they haven't had to struggle with anything as difficult as I have.

—a seventeen–year–old boy

Every parent wants their children to reach a point of acceptance as quickly as possible. What we must remember is that the grieving process is a natural reaction, which must be allowed to run its course. We all have the tendency to believe we're a little farther along than we actually are. So it is with our children. We want to believe that everything is fine, but we usually are premature in our belief that the adjustments are over. This was the case for the Logan family.

Mr. and Mrs. Logan had separated only months prior to my beginning counseling with their children. Mrs. Logan brought them to me early in the separation—not because there were significant problems, but because she wanted to head off some of the more serious difficulties. She hoped that, as a family, they could recover as quickly as possible.

The early intervention seemed to be a big help. Mr. and Mrs. Logan were able amicably to resolve a custody and visitation agreement. Consistently for both of them, their chief concern was the welfare of their three children. In joint sessions with the whole family, the children were informed of the arrangements and assured that they were loved by both parents.

This concerted effort paid off in that both parents and children were spared the depth of anger and fighting that most fractured families experience. The children expressed only a little denial early on, and then went through a period of anger about their situation that I would categorize as mild.

Within a period of months, all three children seemed to be adapting to their new lifestyle. There was very little resentment or depression. In fact, the children were encouraging both Mom and Dad to go out and find someone new. Mom spoke to me at that point about concluding their counseling, since everything seemed to be going so well.

Unfortunately, within a week of that conversation, things began to fall apart. It started with the oldest son Mike, who was about fourteen. The school contacted the mother because they were concerned about Mike's "lack of effort in school, and increasing social withdrawal." On further investigation by the school psychologist, it was concluded that Mike was experiencing significant depression and was in need of counseling.

The other two children began to have a similar reaction. All three were back in counseling. This time we talked about their feelings of loss and sadness. They felt little energy for anything as trivial as schoolwork, and now were very upset whenever Mom went out. They seemed to need additional support and security at home, at a time when Mom was making her own adjustments to a new job and new lifestyle.

We were all a little surprised at how long the feelings of sadness persisted. It seemed like every time things started to improve, some disappointment or disruption would set everyone back a bit. This up–and–back–again growth toward acceptance lasted a full year before the children truly began to get over their grieving.

Today, some two years later, the children have moved on with their lives. They are dealing honestly with the trauma of their parents' divorce.

This does not mean that there are not some difficult moments around the holidays, or that they
don't get mad at Mom or Dad from time to time.
These things happen in all families. But now the
difference is that the children have the emotional
energy to handle each new situation and to face
honestly the implications it will have on their
lives. This is called acceptance.

It is important to remember that you need to
count on at least a two–year recovery time, even
when the situation is amicable and parents provide a helpful support system. The amount of time
for recovery is merely lengthened when parents
refuse to cooperate, but it is rarely shortened
when they do get along.

# DEFENSE MECHANISMS

In terms of the following diagram the acceptance stage is distinguished by the fact that now
your children's defense mechanisms are within
the normal range. Instead of deflecting or distorting, they are able now to allow new information about family or environment to affect them
directly. Most information passes through the defense layers, and then is able to reach the inner
self without alteration. This is the way healthy individuals deal with their world. The defense system is still in place, however, because we all need
protection at times when information is too hurtful to absorb. We continue to filter and distort

# Stage Three: Acceptance

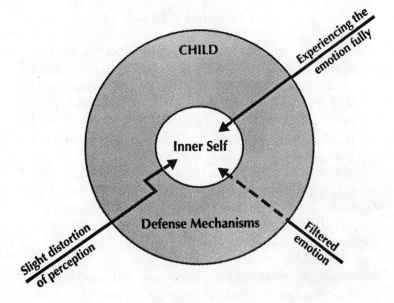

## Attempting to Deal Honestly and Directly with Our Situation

some information for the rest of our lives. When in acceptance, we are able to deal honestly with most input from our world. We learn and grow from the experience. This is known as coping.

How is this theoretical diagram played out practically in my children's lives? Let's examine how the acceptance stage is experienced within specific age groups.

# Preschoolers

In this age group it is unusual for children to reach a point of acceptance. In actuality, most preschoolers merely delay their reactions until they reach a developmental stage in which they can understand what has happened to them and their family. In order for these children to deal honestly with the consequences and ramifications of their parents' divorce, they usually need to wait a few years before they are completely aware of how it will affect their lives. Once they understand that, and come to terms with this realization, then they have reached acceptance.

This is why many children who see their parents split up at such a young age will have a mild reaction within the first couple of years. They may even appear to have no reaction at all. When they reach six or seven years of age, they may go through a modified grieving reaction. It's as if they just realized the extent of the problem. Then, as they enter each new developmental transition (school, teen years, adulthood), they may experience another reaction due to new realizations of the effects of the divorce.

For example, children of two might show little reaction at first. After a period of insecurity and/ or anger, they seem to accept the fact that they live with their mother and visit their father every other weekend.

Once they enter kindergarten or first grade, they realize that their family is different from other families. Perhaps they miss having their dad around, and will once again mourn that loss as they re-process what has happened to them. At this time children will have the ability to grieve more completely; that is, they can actually reach a point of acceptance of their family situation, even though it has not changed in years. A child cannot really mourn loss until they can understand what it is that they have lost.

This does not mean that your children's grieving is over. As we will see in chapter 7, the effects can last a lifetime. Reactions can range from mild to severe whenever these children prepare to enter a new stage of their lives. The transition from preteen to teen years can provide a whole new set of insecurities. Teen years to adulthood can require additional support needs.

When they begin to think about marriage, or having children, there is a whole new set of questions and adjustments that usually emerge. These adjustments, however, are well beyond the scope of your children's immediate reaction to your divorce. These are considered long–term adjustments, and will be discussed more fully in the next chapter.

# School–aged Children

For school–aged children there is an increasing awareness of the extent of the loss in their lives. So there is an increasing ability to reach a point of acceptance. This does not mean that some of the children who witness their parents' breakup while in this age range do not have a delayed reaction. Some do. However, many are able to reach acceptance within a couple of years, and then honestly handle the mini-crises as they occur throughout their lives.

At the lower end of this age range (ages six to eight), children will return to youthful play, fantasy daydreaming, and childlike trust as part of their acceptance. At the upper age range (ages eight to twelve), you will see these children, particularly the girls, begin to take on increased responsibilities. At times, they act very adult–like. It is important that you keep in mind that they are still children. You may be tempted to treat them like adults, giving them more responsibilities, expecting mature decision–making, and maybe even confiding in them. Foster their independence, but don't fall into the trap of robbing them of their childhood.

Other signs of acceptance within this age range can include: a restoration of self–confidence and personal security, a return to normal scholastic achievement, the ability to focus on new and/or renewed friendships, and an acceptance of the new family structure so that few emotional adjustments occur when your former spouse visits or calls. Within all of these changes, the key ingredient is the fact that your children are now able to cope with the changes in their lives. They are facing their situation with a sense of acceptance and restored hope.

## Teenagers

For teenagers it is sometimes difficult to recognize when they are in acceptance. This is because they usually are going through so many adjustments and transitions that it is hard to figure out when they are being typical teenagers, and when they are experiencing anger or depression over the divorce. It is not uncommon for this age group to experience a prolonged grieving period. This can last until teenagers come to a point of stability in their lives. When you combine the turbulence of puberty with the trauma of divorce, you can see how acceptance can be elusive.

Some teenagers do make the necessary adjustments. They may continue to struggle and experience pain, but they are able to cope with their new situation. Some of the evidence that this is taking place can include the following.

- Your teenagers are able to talk to you or someone else about what they are experiencing. They are able honestly and accurately to describe the circumstances of the divorce and their emotions.

- For the most part, forgiveness has taken place. Even though your teens may know that one or both parents were at fault, they no longer blame or resent that person.
- Even though your teens may not be able to express their love, there is a reestablishment of a loving relationship. This is one in which a rebuilding of trust is taking place.
- Your teens should show signs of risk–taking, such as reaching out in new relationships. Risk–taking involves facing your fears or insecurities, and moving forward anyway. So knowledge is gained. Parents should notice evidence that some personal growth, as opposed to regression, is taking place.
- There needs to be some sign of personal responsibility before teenagers can be considered to be in acceptance. This does not mean that your children are taking any of the responsibility for the divorce itself. But they need to move beyond blaming their parents or others for most of their problems. Instead, your teens should show signs of beginning to take responsibility for their own actions and reactions. Hopefully they are gaining a sense of control over their recovery process. Since this ability requires higher level reasoning skills, it usually increases as your children develop and mature.

THE ACCEPTANCE STAGE

# Adults

It may seem surprising, but adults experience the same depth of pain and grieving as do the children, when their parents split up. Many parents have told me that they choose to wait until their children are older and perhaps out of the house before separating. They are surprised to find that their children still go through the same grieving process, even though they seemingly were less dependent on their parents.

Assuming their lives are somewhat stabilized, adult children of divorcing parents tend to recover within the two–year time frame and show signs of acceptance more quickly than younger children or teenagers. The list of signs of acceptance is similar if not identical to the list found in the teenage section. The major difference is the amount of time involved. Since adults are better able to understand adult-like motivations and behaviors, they are more apt to accept and forgive *after* they have worked through their own grieving. There is one word of caution, however. Your adult children are much more likely to figure out what really happened, even though you may not tell them. They are less likely to see one parent as right and the other as wrong. They probably see fault on both sides, even though they might side with you when they are in your presence. This is commonly known as buttering both sides of your bread. This is not necessarily negative, since this is a natural reaction to being caught in the middle.

## HELPING YOUR CHILDREN REACH ACCEPTANCE

You can't really speed up the recovery time, but you *can* reduce the pain involved, by making some wise decisions. You can prolong the recovery by making some poor choices; such as, using your children to get back at the other parent, prolonging the hostilities, or dating before you or the children are emotionally ready. These, and many other errors of judgment, are common among parents who are divorcing.

It is important for you to keep in mind that *the greatest predictor of your children's reaching a point of acceptance is for you as a parent to reach acceptance first*. Children typically don't recover in an atmosphere where a parent continues to get angry or fight over co-parenting issues. They also do not do well in an environment where depression, gloom, and hopelessness are pervasive. You need to do whatever it takes to make *yourself* healthy, and then concentrate on helping your children. I have heard parents say to me they couldn't attend to a divorce recovery program because they didn't want to spend the time away from their children. Or, they probably need counseling, but would rather spend the money to get counseling for their children, since their kids are their priority.

Although I admire the intention of these parents, I also know that it doesn't help the children to work on recovery issues and then walk into a home atmosphere where there is an unforgiving spirit. Acceptance needs to be modeled to kids from their parents first.

This does not mean that you cannot show weakness or vulnerability with your children. In fact, some signs of healthy grieving can be very helpful to kids. One single mother recently told me about her struggle not to cry in front of her children. She wanted to appear strong and healed, even though she was working through a lot of sorrow.

I told her that I thought it would be good for her to let her children see her cry. "They need to see the healthy expression of emotion, and to know that it is okay. On the other hand," I continued to explain to her, "you don't want to demonstrate hysterical, uncontrolled crying. The kids can benefit from seeing you struggle a bit, but they also need to know that you are still in control —at least in control enough for them to feel secure in their dependence on you."

Honesty seems to be a key in the expression of your emotions with your children. Explain to them how you are feeling and where you are in the recovery process. Don't tell them you are in acceptance when you know you are not. You don't want to lie to yourself or to your children about how you are feeling emotionally.

You may, however, want to push yourself a bit for the sake of the kids. By this I mean, you may want to give in or give up some of your own problems, so that everyone involved can get on with their lives. This is good for you as well as the children.

A good example of this would be the Morgan family. There is no question about the fact that Mrs. Morgan had been dumped. She had put her husband through medical school, and now that he was a prominent doctor, he had left his wife for a younger woman. This is an unfortunate, yet all too common, scenario. I can certainly empathize with Mrs. Morgan's hostility and desire for vindication. Yet when she and her children arrived at my office some two years after the breakup, I was struck by how destructive *both* parents had been to their children. They had returned to court several times over custody and financial battles. And now, once again, Mrs. Morgan was thinking of going to court for more support.

After talking extensively with her two children, I recognized that they had both suffered extreme heartache because of their being used as pawns in most of the legal battles. Even though their parents desired to leave them out of it, the kids inevitably heard the venom that each side was going to use during the next legal round.

## THE ACCEPTANCE STAGE

Acknowledging the amount of time that had passed, and the devastating effects on the children, I recommended that the mother examine her motives for going back into court, and try to avoid the litigation. As we discussed the matter further, it became obvious to both of us that she needed to let go of her need to make her husband pay. In turn, I assured her that both she and her children would be better off.

As you move on with your life, and especially if things begin to go well, you will begin to recognize the value in forgiving your ex. Forgiveness is necessary, whether or not the other party asks for it. In fact, there is almost never a time when the erring party comes back with his or her tail between their legs, requesting that you forgive them. That only happens in your dreams. The truth is that we need to forgive the other party in spite of their actions toward us, because this is what truly sets us free to move on with our lives. For the sake of our children, we need to move on! (See the appendix on divorce recovery.)

The true test of forgiveness comes when you're not doing well, and it seems like your ex is prospering. Then, even the most kindhearted soul steams inside, fantasizing about how they might hasten their ex-spouse's downfall. I'm reminded of the single parent who told me that she loaded her kids up with sugar and caffeine before sending them over to visit with their dad and his new wife! (I hope I haven't given any of you new ideas.)

Since it is inevitable that these feelings will continue to haunt you, your decision to forgive must be ongoing. You must choose continually to ignore or let go of nagging concerns and pitfalls. Your children will see how you handle minor crises that come up, and they will learn appropriate responses to life's traumas.

## CHAPTER SUMMARY

In this chapter we have looked at the final stage of adjustment that children of divorce experience: acceptance. This last stage can take two years or more to reach. We have defined this stage as the point at which your children are able to deal honestly with their new lifestyle, and begin to move forward in new and more healthy directions. This adjustment is different within various age groups, but is universally marked by children's ability to be satisfied with their new family. Their defenses are lowered, and they are able to begin taking risks again in significant relationships.

Once your children reach acceptance, this does not mean they will not slip back into another period of adjustment. In fact, it is typical, particularly for younger children, to go through all of the stages of grieving each time they approach a new developmental stage, or a significant transition in their lives. This is considered by many to be a delayed reaction, or to be just part of the long–term effects of the divorce. These long–term effects will be the subject of our next chapter.

# LONG–TERM EFFECTS

Cindy had problems with relationships. She had broken off four serious relationships in two years. For each of them, the pattern was always the same. Cindy would grow closer and closer, until some type of commitment was implied. Then the difficulties would start. The specifics were different each time, but the basic issues were always the same.

According to Cindy her partners couldn't be trusted. She would usually set up some type of trap in which she tested the character of her boyfriend. Sometimes it would be checking his whereabouts, even though he told her where he would be. Other times it was merely whether or not he could account for all of his time when asked, "What did you do today?"

I can remember one specific incident in which Cindy was incensed by her boyfriend's so-called dishonesty. It seems that when she asked him about what he had done that day, he failed to mention that he had called for her earlier in the evening and talked briefly with her roommate. Cindy suspected there was something going on between her boyfriend and her roommate. Needless to say, the relationship did not last much longer, and her friendship with her roommate became strained.

Cindy, who is now twenty-five years old, came to counseling to find out why she seemed to have such poor luck in relationships. As you may have guessed, Cindy came from a divorced home. She first found out about her father's indiscretions when she was about ten. Her parents did not divorce right away. But Cindy remembers a series of incidents in which her mom and dad had prolonged arguments over suspected affairs. Finally, when she was seventeen, Cindy's parents got a divorce. Her mom continually reminded Cindy about how devious her father had been, even though Cindy still saw him a couple of times a month.

This is a typical example of a divorce that has long–term implications. Today we are seeing more and more published about the long–term effects of divorce on individuals. In one of the more popular works on this topic, Judith Wallerstein followed children of divorce for over fifteen years. (See the appendix on adult children of divorce.) This book, along with many followup articles and books, seems to have given adult children of divorce the courage to come forward to tell their stories. The comments I hear repeatedly proclaim, "I'm glad someone is finally recognizing and documenting the long–term effects of divorce. It has had a significant impact on our lives and relationships." One of the greatest proofs of the impact of divorce on children is found in talking to the adult children of divorce. Every one of them, and I've talked to hundreds, has said, "I'll do everything I can to be sure I don't do this to my children." The sad truth is that children of divorce actually have a slightly higher divorce rate than the rest of the population.

Many of you probably are aware of the interest there is today in establishing support groups for those who have come from dysfunctional families. These groups most frequently include adult children of alcoholics and adult children of incest and abuse. Now, more and more, we are seeing adult children of divorce as one of the recovery groups offered. (See the appendix on adult children.) At our own counseling center, just the mention of such a support group will usually initiate many calls of interest from potential participants. As one caller recently stated, "I know my parents' divorce, and the following years of conflict, have affected me. I'm not quite sure of all of the ways I have been affected, but I'd love to talk to others who have been through the same type of experience. Just to know that I'm not alone in my feelings, and to gain insights into some of my behaviors, would be well worth it."

# LONG–TERM VS. SHORT–TERM

Many ask, "What's the difference between the long–term and short–term effects of divorce?" The short–term effects of divorce are those reactions that begin immediately and can last for a number of years. The short–term reactions don't truly end, however, until the children reach a point of acceptance. Beyond that, even though the children have worked through the grieving of their family breakup, they still have to work through the implications of growing up in a divorced home. These effects, which are what I consider to be the long–term effects, have been documented to last up to fifteen years for some adult children of divorce, and may very well be permanent.

In chapter 3, when I discussed the three main categories of reaction for children, I mentioned that approximately one–third of the children of divorce never seem to recover from the trauma of their parents' divorce. These are the most seriously affected children of divorce, both from long–term and short–term perspectives. For these children, the reactions included in chapters 4 through 6 are what they tend to live with for the rest of their lives. They don't learn healthy coping skills, and lead lifestyles of continuing struggle, depression, anxiety, and difficulty in personal relationships.

The children, who after a period of adjustment are able to cope and move on with their lives, are the ones who seem normal to those around them, and outwardly lead healthy, productive lives. Yet as is true for all of us, what they grew up with has a considerable effect on how they live today. Divorce shapes our personalities and characters, our interests and ambitions. These are the subtle changes that will be covered as part of the long–term effects of divorce on children. As might be expected, this will only be a general review of the research, and a personal review of my experiences. Time and practicality do not permit us to discuss all of the subtle changes that take place with your children. You can observe your own children to see how they change over time.

# FACTORS TO BE CONSIDERED

There are a number of factors to be considered when discussing how your children will be affected over the long–term. Let me list a few of the more prevalent factors.

*1. The age of the children at the time of the divorce.* Researchers estimate that most of your children's personalities are developed by the age of six. This does not mean that there are not changes in their personalities beyond that time. But for those children who witness their parents' breakup at a young age, there is a greater chance that it will have an effect on their personalities. The longer your children live in a single-parent or blended family, the more likely it will affect their personalities. This does not have to be a frightening statistic for those of you who have young children. It merely indicates that you will need to be even more aware of how your children might be affected, and how you might compensate for specific losses. (Note: Most of the long-term studies have started with young children, and may be overly pessimistic, since these children spent a greater percentage of their lives in a divorced home.)

2. *The number of changes that result from the divorce.* The impact of divorce on children is greater when you add other life stresses; such as, a new home, new church, new school district, new spouse, or a blended family. All of these changes are difficult for children if they are experienced on separate occasions. But when they are heaped together, as is the case in many divorcing situations, the effects can be lifelong. Wherever possible, parents need to control the number of changes, and perhaps even make sacrifices in order to limit the upheaval.

3. *The adjustment of the custodial parent in the divorce.* While both parents are of key importance in the eventual well-being of the children, research indicates that the emotional health of the custodial parent (usually the mother) is the great-

est predictor of the children's adjustment. It is important for both parents to get the help they need to resolve the anger, resentment, depression, or anxiety produced by the divorce, and to conclude any ongoing squabbles as quickly as possible. Almost all couples have conflicts during the early stages of divorce. But if these continue beyond the actual divorce settlement, they can suck all participants back into the black hole of divorce for more years than necessary.

Since children spend the majority of their time with the custodial parent, it stands to reason that parental attitudes will influence the children. No matter what the circumstances, the custodial parent must choose an attitude of reconciliation and desire to do whatever is best for the children, particularly when it comes to the relationship with the other parent.

*4. The relationship with the noncustodial parent.* For years we have tended to ignore the importance of the relationship with the noncustodial parent (usually the father). Within the past five years or so, we have seen more and more research which points to the fact that the noncustodial parent is also a key player. (Any of you dads out there who might be thinking about giving up on seeing your kids, please read this carefully.) Many researchers have found that a primary reason for negative effects of divorce on children was the loss of contact with one of the parents (usually Dad). And in fact, the traditional visiting pattern of every other weekend has created feelings of intense dissatisfaction, and at times reactive depression, among children, particularly the boys.

Consistent and frequent contact with the non-custodial parent has repeatedly been shown to correlate with well–adjusted children, unless the father is abusive or otherwise unfit. The relationship with the father has been linked to identity with the opposite sex for girls, ambition and motivation for boys, and overall adjustment and relating abilities for both sexes. The well–being of the children has proven to be particularly strong when the custodial mother encourages the continued contact with the father.

If the relationship with the noncustodial parent is so important, then why is it that two years after the divorce only 40 percent of the fathers have regular visits with their children? This is an alarming and discouraging statistic. Having talked with many fathers who have actually given up, I have found that many become discouraged by their lack of input into the children's upbringing. To put it in their words, "Why should I continue paying, when I have little or no say in how the kids are raised?" Perhaps this is the reason joint custody arrangements have a much higher rate of involvement by the father. When they have more input, they are more likely to stay involved, and more likely to have well–adjusted children.

5. *Other specific traumas that accompany the divorce.* Research for this is incomplete, but it is my

opinion that most of the children of divorce, who fall into the one–third of the children who never seem to recover from their parents' divorce, are also the ones who have to contend with other specific traumas. These traumas include, but are not limited to, physical abuse, sexual abuse, severe emotional or verbal abuse, extended neglect, drug or alcohol addiction of one or both parents, and mental illness in the family. For children exposed to these factors, the long–term implications of divorce are greatly complicated by preexisting conditions and compounding problems. This is a general statement, and does not imply that if your children were exposed to one or more of these traumas, they will end up basket cases. This factor merely indicates a greater propensity for long–term problems. You need to be particularly sensitive to your children's needs and emotional condition.

## LONG–TERM EFFECTS

Jason, who is now twenty-four, first came to see me when he was fifteen. At that time he had long hair, torn jeans, a punk rock T-shirt, and a sour look on his face. Jason was actually referred to me by his mom because he had decided to drop out of school. Mom said she would permit it (she had actually lost her ability to control him anymore), if he would go to three counseling sessions.

Imagine yourself in my position. Here's this big, fifteen–year–old punk rocker, sitting in your office glaring at you, as if to say, "I dare you to get through to me." He didn't want to be there. To be honest, I didn't either.

Every topic I brought up was met with silence, or an occasional "yep" or "nope" (mostly "nope's"). Finally, I decided that my only option, and one that I found would work as a last resort, was to talk to him about something *he* was interested in: music. This was not just any music, but punk rock and heavy metal music. Now you have to understand that I detest punk rock or heavy metal music. In fact, I encourage parents to keep it away from their kids. But in this case, I felt it was my only way to connect.

Suddenly Jason became very animated and talkative. He was surprised that I had shown any interest. (Believe me, it was tough.) He later stated that no other adult had ever taken an interest in this topic, which he valued so highly. Adults usually walked away or told him to turn it off (both the music *and* his conversation about it). Jason went on to tell me about all the groups, the most popular songs, and the meaning behind the lyrics. (As if anyone could actually hear the words.) He offered to bring his tape player next week, along with a couple of his favorite cassettes.

I survived his tapes, and Jason continued coming, by choice, for the next six months. During that time, he began to tell me about his family, his life, and his feelings. Jason was a very angry young man. His father had left home when he was about nine years old, and moved in with another woman. The new woman had children of her own, and was soon pregnant with Jason's soon–to–be stepbrother. As Dad gradually broke off contact (and financial support) with his former family, Jason felt more rejection, resentment, and anger with each passing week. He eventually withdrew emotionally, and isolated himself in his room with his music and an occasional marijuana cigarette.

Jason's main problems were his attitude and motivation. He had given up on life by the time he was fourteen. After all, life wasn't fair, and he couldn't even sustain his father's love. This inability to have a sense of control over his own life is what researchers have identified in approximately 45 percent of the male children of divorce. As in the case of Jason, even though children might be intelligent and talented, there is a higher tendency for them to show little direction or purpose in their lives. Dropping out of school, not attending college, and being under–employed, are all typical signs of the phenomenon in the male, and a few female, children of divorce.

Today, Jason works in a factory. He finished high school, but went no farther even though he has above–average intelligence. He is socially active, and appears to be much happier today. His hair is still long. (Fortunately his taste in music has moderated.) To his friends, he's an average

twenty–four–year–old. But to me, he is a victim—
a victim of divorce.

Alice is a twenty–six–year–old adult child of divorce. Her parents split up when she was seven,
and she gradually lost contact with her father
over two years. Her mother remarried within that
time, but was divorced again when Alice was
eleven. Since the second divorce, Alice's mom has
had a series of boyfriends, but has not remarried
again. After a period of adjustment, Alice seemed
to come through both divorces fairly well. It was
in adolescence, as is often the case, that Alice began to have difficulties. She found her first "true
love" when she was fifteen, and was convinced
they would eventually marry. When that relationship broke off, Alice found, in disgust, that she
could get boys to do what she wanted them to do,
by offering sexual favors. Throughout high school
and college, Alice was sexually active, but soon
after graduation had a born–again experience,
which led her into a new lifestyle. She became
active in a church singles group. She now believes in a heavenly Father who loves her uncon-
ditionally, and for whom she does not have to
perform. The new difficulty is in finding that same
kind of loving relationship with an eligible man.

Whether it is the reaction found in Alice, or the
lack of trust found in the example of Cindy (from
the first paragraph of this chapter), researchers
have documented this sleeper effect in approximately 66 percent of the female children of divorce. This has been called the sleeper effect be-

cause it has been found quite often in the women who previously seemed to be well–adjusted. It occurs most frequently at a time when women are making important decisions about their lives.

The common element in the sleeper effect, as seen in the two women presented, is fear—fear of commitment and fear of betrayal. For some, fear may lead to the coping strategy of control. "If I can learn how to control men, or the situation, then I won't be hurt again." I have seen this numerous times in the lives of adult children. While I can empathize with the feeling, I'm afraid the coping strategy can become quite unhealthy.

Another coping strategy, which is used by both men and women who are experiencing the sleeper effect, is avoidance. This can include avoidance of significant relating, or avoidance of any kind of commitment. Usually patterns of relating are developed, and unconsciously repeated, in which relationships only reach a certain level, and then self–destruct before they can go any farther. This pattern includes inability to communicate deeper than at a superficial level, inability to make a commitment, or inability to allow the relationship to grow beyond a friendship or a purely sexual basis.

The combination of control and avoidance can reach extreme levels among some adult children of divorce. This is evidenced by a disproportionately high number of both men and women who experience divorce in their own marriages in spite of vows that it will never happen to them.

Without insights into their pattern of relating, and help in overcoming these patterns, these difficulties may follow them the rest of their lives.

Another documented long–term effect of divorce is commonly referred to as the over–burdened child. When marriage breaks down, it is common for both the mother and the father to do less parenting. The mother, or custodial parent, is often worn down by the changes in her life, including moves, job changes, new financial responsibilities, and parenting alone. The father, who feels guilt because he is not there for the kids as often as he'd like to be, just wants their times together to be enjoyable. So both parents tend to discipline less, spend less time with their children, and may be less sensitive to their needs. The adults may be struggling with their own reactions and recovery.

Unable to meet the challenges of parenting as a single, many parents begin to lean on their children to pick up the slack. We have all heard of latchkey kids, who must take major responsibilities in the home well before they might otherwise have to. The children's roles may include housekeeping, babysitting younger siblings, being the man of the house, becoming the mediator in arguments, being the parent's confidant, and emotionally supporting the parent. While most of this is not intentional, it is a fact of life in many single–parent families.

The first time I met Sarah, I was amazed at what a responsible, mature child she was for fourteen. Her mother was proud of the fact that teachers and friends all commented on what a good job she had done in raising her daughter alone. The present problem was that they were having difficulty in choosing a college. Even though it was early, Sarah was anticipating a problem when it came time for her to go away to school. You see, she wanted to go *away* for school. Her mother, on the other hand, felt that Sarah should stay home so that she, the mother, could continue to provide the proper guidance to her daughter.

Since college was still three years away, and Sarah was so responsible, I was confused about why this was such a burning issue. As we explored it further, it became evident that the reason Mom needed Sarah to stay home was to help Mom keep it together. Sarah was the one who kept the house in order. She prepared the evening meal, and then would ask Mom all about her day when she got home from work. Sarah did not go out socially during the week or on weekends because she didn't want her mother to be alone at home. If Mom did happen to go out on a date, which was rare, she always solicited Sarah's approval on her choices. "Sarah," she stated, "is a better judge of character than I am."

Whenever she returned from a date, she would confide in Sarah everything that she liked and didn't like about the person so that together they could come to some conclusion about any future relationship. The truth of the matter was that if

Sarah went away to college, neither one of them were sure if Mom could make it on her own. What a role reversal!

Sarah is a good example of the overburdened child. The children's role becomes instrumental in maintaining the well–being of the parent. The divorce itself may not be to blame, but serves as a catalyst for bringing to the surface specific emotional difficulties. As with any type of dysfunctional family, the results of the children taking on so much responsibility, so early in life, is generally twofold. Either they react by going the opposite way and become overly irresponsible, or they continue in their overburdened lifestyle, and are at risk for perfectionism, nervous breakdowns, overly nurturing relationships, overparenting, and losing their own identity for a cause or another person. (See the appendix on codependency.)

Preliminary studies have indicated that approximately 15 percent of the children of divorce are overburdened. Some have indicated that this estimate is low, since there are increased responsibilities for nearly all children of divorce. As we shall see in the next section, a balance of responsibility may be the key, since increased responsibility can actually have a positive impact on some children of divorce.

Whether it is diminished motivation, the sleeper effect, or the overburdened child syndrome, it is hard only to point the finger of blame at divorce. Divorce never stands alone as a one–

time traumatic event, but is experienced on a continuum. It begins with an unhappy marriage, goes through custody battles and court hearings, and begins ripple effects that continue for generations. The biblical phrase from Exodus 20 comes to mind: "The sins of the father are passed on through many generations."

Do these predictions of gloom mean that parents should stay together for the sake of the children? Even though research is troubling and needs to be taken seriously, there are situations in which continuing the marriage would be intolerable. And to stay in a bad situation for the sake of the children would probably only lead to more resentment, and possible violence. Even though there are few comparisons of children from divorced homes with children from unhappy homes, all known evidence points to the fact that children exposed to parental fighting and the pressure of relentless conflict turn out to be less well–adjusted than many of the children of divorce.

If divorce is undertaken with thoughts of the children's well–being, and if both parents work together for the sake of the kids, then there are many things that can be done to lessen the negative effects on your children. These practical guidelines will be the focus of the next section of this book. But first let's turn our attention to a much more positive topic.

# POSITIVE EFFECTS

It is hard to believe that anything positive could be written about divorce. In fact, in reviewing the literature, it is hard to find anything positive. But if divorce is viewed as a handicap to children, then we must consider the fact that many have taken the worst kinds of handicaps and used them to build character and personality, which become the envy of others. So it is with the long–term effects of divorce. I have met many teenagers and adults who have shared how their parents' divorce has built strength of character and moral resolve. Janet, a sixteen–year–old child of divorce, explained it to me.

> It is hard to find anything positive that can come out of the divorce when it first happens. My dad left when I was only six, and I know that it has been difficult on me and my mom. But I wouldn't trade anything for the things that I have learned from growing up in a single–parent household. I was forced to face the realities of life at an early age. Realities, like "life isn't always easy," and "there are no guarantees," have forced me to be more practical and down to earth. I know that I'm a more responsible and resourceful person today because of the divorce.

Crystal, a seventeen–year–old, echoed similar comments.

It definitely takes time, but you do work through it. When you do, you find that you are much more understanding than other kids your age. You have to be! After all, you've seen your parents fail. Everything they taught you has fallen apart. So now you have to decide how you're going to live your life, what you are going to believe in. For me, it has strengthened my faith in God. He is real in my life, not because my parents told me so, but because I needed a source of strength that was greater than I could be on my own, and greater than my parents. I've found that now, so I consider myself luckier than other kids my age.

David, a seventeen–year–old survivor of two divorces, put it this way.

Something about the divorce forces you to view life differently. It somehow puts every other life event in perspective. When your mom or dad leaves you at age five, and your whole world seems to fall apart, then you are better able to deal with other crises as they occur. You're wiser and more mature. I see some of my classmates who fall apart over bad grades or college entrance exams or something. You even read about kids who kill themselves because they didn't get accepted to the college of their choice. Things like that upset me, but I know it's not the end of the world. I always figure I've survived my parents' divorce, I can certainly get through this one.

Here are some of the common themes I have heard when interviewing children of divorce about the positive aspects of divorce. First and foremost, they all indicate that there is nothing good about it in the beginning. But over a long period of time, some of the following characteristics may emerge.

*1. Children of divorce are more sensitive to other kids and their problems.* When you've been through a significant life trauma and have felt like no one else understands your pain, you are bound to be more compassionate toward other people and the difficulties they might face. I have seen this firsthand whenever our counseling center sponsors a program to help others who are struggling with some life crisis. Adult and teenage children of divorce are among the first to volunteer to help.

Julie, a sixteen–year–old girl, expressed it like this:

> Having cried myself to sleep many times, I realize the depth of pain a little girl can feel. Now, when I have the opportunity to share my healing with someone else who is struggling, I feel like it was almost worth it. A lot of my friends come to me with their problems, because they say I understand them and can really relate. You know, I think

they're right. But it's taken a long time for me to get to the point where I can help anyone.

2. *Children of divorce tend to be more mature and responsible than their peers.* Even though this maturity comes from the school of hard knocks, many of the children of divorce that I have spoken with seem to have a wisdom beyond their years. This comes from having to grapple with issues that other kids don't have to face until they are much older—issues like loyalty, betrayal, adultery, child support, court hearings, and rejection. Although you would probably prefer to have your children avoid these issues, they do help children move from concrete to abstract reasoning.

One teenage boy put it this way:

> I used to just think about me and my needs. Now I'm more concerned about my little brother. I've tried to support him through this mess, because I know how much I hurt when I was his age. I sometimes just take him fishing, or something, so we can get away and talk. We cry together, laugh together. We're closer now than ever.

Since your children inevitably take on more responsibilities, either they fight the changes, or eventually become more responsible people. They stop blaming, or looking to others for the solution to their problems, and realize that they've got to take responsibility for their own futures. Many people don't learn this until they are adults. But the pressure cooker of divorce has a way of maturing children more quickly than might otherwise be expected.

Margie, a seventeen–year–old, said:

> Before the divorce, my life was fairly secure. Everything was taken care of as far as my schooling, my welfare, and even my future. Then, when everything fell apart, I learned that the world wasn't secure at all. While in high school I had to work, take care of my brothers and sisters, cook and clean. I feel like I got a taste of motherhood. I'm leaving for college soon, and I know that I'm going to have to work my way through. But I know I'll value my education more, and not take things for granted as much. After all, it's my education and my future.

This increased level of responsibility may include the children's moral development. Children of divorce are faced with their parents' moral failures—lies, manipulations, maybe even cheating and stealing. Obviously, this forces children to think more about what they believe and how they are going to live their lives. It is no longer enough to believe something because "my mother told me so."

After a sometimes rebellious transition, children of divorce settle down to a belief system that is based on what they have concluded about life, rather than what their parents have taught them. Even though this may be a scary thought to parents, it is actually a more mature and enduring belief system. Nancy explained it this way:

> All my life my parents taught me right and wrong. Then I saw my mom and dad break just about every one of their own rules. It forced me to really examine what was truth. Today, I have a strong faith in God, which helps me in every area of my life.

*3. Children of divorce are better able to put life experiences into proper perspective.* John said it this way:

> When you've been through some of the worst things at age eight that can happen in life, everything else that comes your way seems so much easier. You've survived divorce, and now you're determined that nothing else is going to get you down again. I still have difficult times, but I always go back to my parents' divorce and compare it to that. Then I know I'm going to be just fine.

Growing up in a storybook life many times leaves us with the expectation that we are going to "live happily ever after." It can be a real shock when we discover that the fairy tale is not true. I have seen adults come apart because they were not prepared for the realities of life, realities that children of divorce learn much earlier. Even though we would rather shield our kids from such difficulties, they have a way of teaching lessons that last a lifetime.

*4. Children of divorce are very motivated to succeed in marriage.* Having experienced firsthand the effects of divorce, children usually are determined that it won't happen to them. Even deeper than this determination is the realization that you can't take certain things for granted, such as someone's love.

Having grown up in a happy, secure home environment, it wasn't until after college when I learned that the world isn't always a fair place and that bad things *do* happen to good people. This was a difficult lesson, which many of us learned after stumbling into relationships with people whom we thought were trustworthy and good. Children of divorce learn at a very young age that good people (their parents) still hurt them, and perhaps can't be trusted. When looking for a mate, they tend to be much more cautious.

Children of divorce (especially women) tend to delay marriage because of their fear of betrayal. This may be healthy, if we consider that they may avoid a future divorce by not marrying the first man they fall in love with. In fact, there is some preliminary evidence in Judith Wallerstein's longitudinal study which suggests that even though children of divorce are afraid of commitment, they eventually settle into relationships that last. She says, "I'm predicting that after a lot of trial and error, after a lot of getting hurt, a significant number of children of divorce will find a relationship that will stick."

When I interviewed teenagers of divorce for this book, I asked the question, "How do you think your future will be affected, particularly your getting married?" Every one of them responded that they would be more cautious about whom they chose to marry. This usually included a list of qualities that they would need to see. One teen put it this way: "I don't mean to be picky, but I am certain I want to know someone for a long time before I marry them. I want to be sure they're not going to change later on. I want someone who is kind and compassionate. But most important, I want someone who has a strong faith in God and knows the meaning of commitment."

One parent summed this point up best: "If my divorce helps to keep my daughter from having to go through the same thing someday, then it was worth it!"

## CHAPTER SUMMARY

In this chapter we have taken a look at some of the long–term effects, both positive and negative, of divorce on children. We have seen some of the important factors that determine your children's adjustment over the long–term. We have made some suggestions to both moms and dads on how they can affect their own children's healthy recovery. Even though there are probably hundreds of ways in which the children's personality is affected by divorce, we took a specific look at three of the most commonly cited effects. These included a lack of motivation and direction in the lives of approximately 40 percent of the young men whose parents divorced; difficulty in relationships among approximately 66 percent of the young women in the study; and an overburdened–child syndrome found in about 15 percent of adult children of divorce.

While these effects are troubling to read about, we also examined some of the positive outcomes that can result from a divorce. The strength of character and resiliency, which have been demonstrated by many children of divorce, are an encouragement and challenge to us all.

As we move into the next section, which deals with helping your children recover in the most healthy way, we all need to remember the part of the Serenity Prayer that states, "God, grant me . . . the courage to change the things I can. . . ."

**SECTION III**

# HELPING
## YOUR
### CHILDREN

# BREAKING THE NEWS

I was five or six when I first remember my parents fighting a lot. I remember that Dad was working more and more, and that I missed him. There were times when Dad was gone for weeks at a time. When we asked my mom where Dad was, she would always say, "Away on a business trip." I now know that my dad and mom were separated. Whenever they tried to reconcile, Mom would say that Dad was home for a vacation.

This went on for about two years. It didn't matter what my mom said anymore. My brother and I knew there was something wrong, and we knew that we didn't like it. When Mom finally told us the truth, that she and Dad were getting a divorce, it was only because he was getting married to someone else, and wanted my brother and me to be in the wedding.

I wish my mom had told us the truth two years earlier. Then we could have started the grieving process, and maybe been more accepting of our new stepmother and stepsister. That was really tough for us to swallow.

—a fourteen–year–old boy

You want to begin to intervene with your children as soon as the possibility of divorce is apparent. For most of you, it is already too late to undo the way the news was broken to your children. But, if possible, this is where you and your spouse will want to start. Kids usually know that there is something going on long before you give them credit for such knowledge. It is also my experience that they know and understand more than you think.

The example at the beginning of this chapter obviously is not the way to break the news to your children. But it is hard to tell each one of you how to handle your particular situation. This section on helping your children will tend to sound like a list of do's and don'ts. Keep in mind that I am presenting guidelines—some of which you can implement, and some of which you can't or won't want to.

Remember our prayer: "God, grant me the serenity to accept the things I cannot change, the courage to change the things I can, and the wisdom to know the difference." Also keep in mind that there are no secret formulas, or even standard methods of operation. Your children are individuals, so you will need to tailor this information to fit your situation, and your children.

# SPEAK THE TRUTH IN LOVE

In the book of Ephesians, the Apostle Paul writes that we are to "speak the truth in love." This is the best way I can describe the communication that should take place between all parties involved in a separation or divorce. This may be nearly impossible at times, but I believe it needs to be our goal. Let's explore how this guideline plays itself out, by answering some of the most commonly asked questions I hear from divorcing parents.

### When should we tell the kids?

It is important to tell the kids what is going on as soon as both of you know. If you're having marital problems, then it is important that you get help, but don't feel compelled to tell the children anything of a personal nature between you and your spouse. If the children are older, then they will know that something is not right, and may even know that you are seeing a counselor. If they ask, use this as an opportunity to demonstrate the proper way to handle problems. "Your mother and I are having some personal problems that we need to work out. Because we are committed to each other and to the family, we want to get help in resolving these problems as quickly as we can." If your children are too young to understand, or if they don't ask, then there is no need to share your personal lives with your kids.

Once you reach a point where divorce or separation is apparent, then it affects the whole family. As soon as it can be arranged, the children need to be told. This should only be delayed if you need to work out some of the details, or if it happens to fall on an important day, such as Christmas or one of the children's birthdays. It is reasonable to wait until at least some of the questions are answered. "Where will Mom live? Where will Dad live? Where will the kids stay? How often will they see each parent?" You need to present a scenario that is thought through and reassuring to the children. If these matters cannot be settled, and it looks like the children are going to find out, you may need to sit down with them and tell them as much as you do know.

Many parents tend to protect their children from the truth as long as possible. One study found that 80 percent of the preschoolers questioned had received no information about their parents' separation. Parents do a disservice to the children by withholding such information. Withholding merely creates anxiety about the future and distrust toward the parents.

## *How should we tell the kids, and how much should we tell them?*

If possible, both parents should sit down together with the kids, and tell them about the separation or divorce, before one of the parents leaves. If the separation happens abruptly, the parent remaining with the children will need to give them some preliminary information right away. But as soon as it can be arranged, both parents need to get together to tell the children what will happen to the family.

This method is important for several reasons. First, with both parents present, there is the greatest possibility of a balanced and honest presentation. Second, if the children have any questions, they need to address them to the parent who is best able to answer. And third, the united front makes it clear that both parents are in agreement on the decision. This helps to reduce splitting of loyalties, playing of one parent against the other, and creating the fantasy, "My parents will work this out." If one parent is missing, the children are likely to think, "This is what Mom says, but I know that's not what Dad told me."

If one parent is not present, and this is usually the case, then it is important that the parent remember to speak the truth as lovingly as possible. Representing both sides of the issue is difficult when you are so emotionally involved. Even though you are upset with the other parent, you want to let the children know that this is an issue between the *parents*, and that you both still love *them*.

If your children have questions about the other parent's reasons for leaving, try to answer these questions as honestly as possible. Don't attribute motives, or make judgments. Just state what you know to be true, as nicely as you can. For example, don't say, "Your father left because he's irresponsible. He's probably going to be moving in with his girlfriend, and forget all about us." Try this instead: "Your father loves you very much, but doesn't seem to love me. Even though he does not want to live with me anymore, he wants to visit with you whenever he can."

By taking this approach, you will end up better off, even if you have good reason to drag your spouse's reputation through the mud. Remember, your children will know the truth sooner or later, and it would be better for you if they remember you as the one who chose the most loving course.

When deciding how much you should tell the kids, you must take into consideration the developmental level of your children. As someone put it, "Get the key points across, and then allow open discussion. If the children know enough to ask a question, then they're old enough to get an honest answer."

The key points to cover include:

- How did this happen? What are the reasons?

BREAKING THE NEWS

- Do you still love me? Does my mother/father still love me? Am I wanted?
- How will my life be changed? Where will I live, go to school, church, etc?
- Am I part of the reason for the breakup? Could I have done something to avoid this separation/divorce?

It is most important to cover what will happen to the children. Reassure them of your love for them, and be prepared to back it up with actions. Give the children permission to love *both* parents. For preschoolers it is important for you to reassure them that they will be cared for, and then explain the divorce in terms they can understand. For example:

Mommy loves you very much. Daddy loves you very much. You are going to live with me. We will stay in this house, where you will eat, sleep and play, just like you do now. Daddy is going to live in an apartment nearby, so he can come and visit you every week. He will pick you up this Saturday and show you where he lives. You will eat lunch there. Then he will bring you back home. I will be waiting to hear all about your day. We are separating because we don't want to fight anymore. We will all be sad about Daddy leaving. But Mommy and Daddy would be even sadder if Daddy stayed here and we fought a lot.

Children who are elementary age or older need more specific information, particularly about where they will live and what the visitation arrangements will be. They will also require more specifics about what went wrong. You need to be as honest as you can, without discussing sexual problems. If possible, avoid placing blame, since it is true that divorce is rarely all one person's fault.

Don't expect your children to understand your explanations, or to ask all their questions the first time you talk about it. Be prepared to explain the situation and answer questions over and over again. Stress that separation and/or divorce is an adult decision. It was not their fault, nor can they do anything to get the parents back together. (See the appendix on children's books.)

### *What if the truth is particularly ugly or hard to talk about?*

It is easier to deal with what we know than with what we imagine. You need to tell your children the truth in as loving a way as you can. The earlier they hear the truth, the sooner they can start to deal with the problem and begin the healing process.

Use discretion, and consider the ages of the children, when answering personal questions. Remember, if they are old enough to ask the question, they are old enough to hear an honest answer. For example, if Dad is leaving because he has a girlfriend, or he is a homosexual, you may not want to give them all of this information at the first meeting. Soon, however, you need to tell them what is going on. The kids will hear whispers and innuendos, so it is best that they hear the truth from their parents. If possible, the information should come from the spouse with the problem. They should know they are hearing firsthand information, which is usually more reliable. Then give the children the opportunity to discuss openly their questions and concerns.

If the offending spouse is not available, or is not willing to talk with the children, then obviously it falls on the other parent to present as balanced an explanation as possible. If the children still have questions, you may want to offer to let them discuss the issue with a neutral individual. This might be a relative they trust, a counselor at school or church, or anyone they might view as being more objective. Your children may not want to do this, but it is important that you offer. This allows them the opportunity to seek a second opinion without feeling like they are betraying you.

Open communication is one of the key elements in a healthy family. Dysfunctional families are marked by too much interaction (known as enmeshment), too little communication or emotional distancing, and distorted messages, as found in controlling and manipulative families. Healthy interactions allow for open discussion with honest questioning. It invites verification, as when one parent questions their own motives, or encourages the children to get the other parent's point of view.

### What about cases where the children are actually abandoned by one of their parents?

When someone apparently abandons their children, it is difficult to speak the truth in a loving way. This is not only because it is hard to be loving in these situations, but because the truth is rarely known. I don't believe that you can tell the children, "Daddy doesn't love you," or, "Daddy's not coming back." There is much evidence to indicate otherwise. Many parents, both mothers and fathers, who apparently abandon their children, will try later to contact them and reestablish a relationship. In addition, the fact that they left does not prove their lack of love. Studies have shown that many times the departing parent feels so badly about themselves that they believe the most loving thing to do is to get out of their family's life. Their thinking can be so distorted that they feel like the best thing for everyone is that they disappear.

In cases of abandonment, the remaining parent needs to balance their comments so that the children do not have undue hope or despair. "I don't know if your father is coming back or not. We need to go on with our lives as if he will never be back. But you never know; he might realize what he is missing someday, and decide to come back to see you."

Another critical reassurance is the children's lovability. "I don't know if your father loves you or not, but I do know that you are very lovable children. He is not thinking properly right now, and has to work through some problems. But I know that if he ever works through those problems, he will realize what wonderful children you are." Or, "I know your father loves you. He just is not able to express it or show it right now, because he is trying to figure out his own life. This does not change the fact that you are wonderful and lovable children. Your father's problems have nothing to do with you."

### *Aren't children really tougher than we think? In other words, can't they eventually recover, no matter how difficult the truth is to hear?*

Most children are more resilient than we think. But that does not advocate telling all to the kids. Unfortunately, this idea often has been misinterpreted as meaning that children are more mature than we think. As a result, children often are expected to handle the impact of divorce with passive serenity. Kids really are tougher than we think in their ability to handle reality, when their parents take the time to communicate honestly with them. Details seldom are necessary, but honesty is critical.

One of the casualties of divorce is trust. Trust is

destroyed when parents, who once said, "We'll always be here for you," are now telling you that Daddy has moved out. The only way to rebuild your children's trust is through honesty and open communication.

If the truth is too much for your children to handle, they may withdraw or react hysterically. It is natural for parents to back off temporarily, and this is probably best. But don't deny the truth, or indicate that "we might get back together," just to relieve the tension. Eventually, you need to encourage your children to express their feelings. To understand the children's feelings, and to allow them to express their pain, take great courage on the part of the parent. To do so will accelerate acceptance and growth on the part of the children. Further, parents who make the effort to understand and comfort their children usually find that they themselves are comforted.

### How can we expect our children to react when we give them the news?

Your children's reaction will vary according to their developmental level and their personality. But generally you can expect some of the following.

One response is under-reaction. This may be a form of denial and the beginning of the grieving process, as outlined in chapter 4. Don't be surprised when your children say, "Can I go out and play now?"

A second response is preoccupation with egocentric thoughts. For all the reasons outlined in chapter 2, your children may say, "What about my birthday?" Or, "Who's going to take me to Disney World?" These are merely concrete expressions of their fear for the future.

A third response is lack of interest in the details of the divorce. This reaction may be a reflection of the children's inability to comprehend the news, and their fear of talking about it. When you ask them if they have questions, it is not unusual for them to express none at the time. It is important that you follow up your initial discussion with other opportunities for the children to express their concerns.

Whatever your children's reaction, it is critical that you continually reassure them, through every stage of their development, that they are loved by both parents and that the divorce was not their fault. Explaining the separation or divorce to your children cannot really be done in one session. It will require new explanations and reassurances as the children grow and mature. Even as adults, your children will still have lingering questions that they will need to express. Hopefully, you will create an atmosphere for them that encourages their inquiries.

### *What if we've already told the children, but we did it all wrong?*

I don't believe it's ever too late to go back and do it right. Granted, some of the questions have already been answered, or figured out by the kids. But that doesn't mean it wouldn't help to have an open discussion about how they feel about all of the changes. You may think that none of these things is an issue for your kids, because they've never mentioned it. That might be because you've never given them permission to talk about it by opening up the conversation.

If you've done it all wrong by giving the children distorted or unloving information about the other parent, then it is best to admit your wrongs to the children, ask for their forgiveness, correct the wrongs, and vow to be more objective and positive in the future.

If possible, and this might really be asking a lot, contact your former spouse to see if he/she might be willing to have a joint meeting with the children. This could go a long way toward establishing a respectful, cooperative effort in co-parenting the children, which benefits everyone.

## CHAPTER SUMMARY

In this chapter, we have examined how to break the news of separation or divorce to your children. We have answered questions regarding when and what to tell the children. Some suggestions, which have been stressed regarding the parents' communication with their children, are:

- Be honest and open in the way you present the information. Give explanations, not defenses or opinions.
- Focus on what will happen to your children. Assure them of their continued well–being, in spite of difficult transitions.
- Make sure the children understand that they were not the cause of the divorce.
- Give clear and definite statements of mutual love and acceptance. Be prepared to back this up with actions, such as hugs, showing interest in their world, and providing a listening ear.
- Let them know that they can't bring their parents back together. Encourage a realistic view of what life will be like after the divorce.
- Expect that you will have to reinforce this information by initiating discussions with your children at regular intervals throughout their lives.

# RESTRUCTURING THE FAMILY

My whole world was turned upside down when my parents broke up. My mom took my brother and me away from our home to live with our grandparents for a few months. After that we moved into this lousy apartment with no furniture. I had to attend a school that I used to make fun of. They were our rivals in sports, and the kids all seemed like drug addicts. Now I'm in this school, trying to make friends. It's like my worst nightmare come true.

My parents are always arguing about stupid stuff, mostly money, and about when my brother and I are coming over to see Dad. I get tired of being in the middle of it. Mom tells me to ask Dad for the support check when I see him. Then Dad starts yelling at me about how he'd send the check if "your mother would let me see you guys when she is supposed to."

I hate it when my parents talk to each

HELPING YOUR CHILDREN

other, because they always fight. But when
they're not talking, I end up having to send
messages back and forth.

—a sixteen–year–old boy

Restructuring a home and family is always difficult and stressful. When you add the grief and
trauma of a divorce, you have the makings of an
explosive situation. The purpose of this chapter is
to provide guidelines on how to make these
changes with the least turmoil and emotional
harm. One can never eliminate all negative consequences or mistakes. But there is much you as a
parent can do to smooth the transition.

Here are some of the more prevalent problem
areas in the transition from married life to single–
parenting.

# CUSTODY AND
# VISITATION

Other than money issues, there is no other issue more troublesome or emotionally charged
than the custody and visitation rights of each parent. It will not be our focus to discuss the different types of arrangements, because there are too
many variables. For information on your options,
I encourage you to talk with a lawyer, or a divorce mediation specialist. Each state has its own
laws, which vary according to the views of the

judges who oversee such cases. You need to be advised by someone who is familiar with the system, and the way it works in your specific area.

As a psychologist, there is much that I can say about the emotional side of the custody and visitation battle—the first of which would be not to make it a battle. Remember, the more you can resolve amicably among yourselves, the more you will save in money, time, wear and tear on your nerves, and damaging effects to your children. I can't tell you how many times I have heard stories like Lori's.

> My husband and I fought for almost five years over who would get the children. It started out badly, and only got worse with each new round of hearings. By the time we were done, we had used every possible devious tactic and called each other every name in the book. Of course, the children heard it all, and the only winners were the lawyers. Our legal fees were over $40,000, which was more than we had tried to split between us some five years earlier.

Whenever I have a divorcing parent tell me they want to fight the other parent in order to come out on top, I feel compelled to tell them that there are no winners in a divorce, except perhaps for the lawyers. If you think you are going to fight your particular case until you finally win, please rethink what you are doing. You will not win. You merely will run out of resources and energy. At this point you will probably have to compromise to a position which probably you could have obtained much earlier, and at half the expense.

However, there is an exception. In cases of abuse or extreme misconduct on the part of the other parent, you need to fight for the rights of your children. Standing up for your own rights is something I encourage all parents to do. But it is not worth battling the other parent, unless you or your children are in some type of physical or emotional danger.

Since you are not the most objective person to judge whether or not your case falls into the extreme category, I would encourage you to seek third–party objectivity from a neutral advisor. You need to recognize that your friends and relatives are usually biased in your favor, and your lawyer, for obvious reasons, may tend to advocate an adversarial position.

Here are some other guidelines about custody and visitation rights.

Set up a workable visitation arrangement as soon as the separation occurs. This will help the children adjust to a new routine, while assuring continuity with both parents. This also paves the way for a smoother settlement of the official agreement. Keep visitation consistent, so children know what to expect and when they will see the other parent. When unscheduled changes occur, let your children know as soon as possible.

With teenagers, flexibility is needed because of

their busy schedules and outside activities. Both parents should respect the teens' wishes, but not at the expense of the relationship with the other parent. For example, if your teenagers are planning to work on weekends, this must be decided and arranged in consultation with both parents, since it tends to affect the relationship with the noncustodial parent.

Holidays need to be planned well in advance, and then explained to the children. Don't wait until the week before Christmas to talk with the other parent about how vacations are to be handled. This leads to undue stress for parents and children, at a time when you need it the least. Older children and teens may be consulted about their wishes for the holidays. But the final decision must be the parents'.

Unless your children are preschoolers, you should consult with them about the visitation arrangement. This is particularly true of teenagers. Even though you ask them their opinion, make sure they understand that the final decision is up to the parents, and will not be decided by the children. Keep in mind your children's tendency to tell you what they think you want to hear. Expect they will say one thing to you, and something else to the other parent. Don't embarrass or punish them for this. They want the love and loyalty of both parents desperately. Use their wishes as input into your final decision.

If a court case becomes inevitable, try to keep the children out of it. If their testimony is crucial,

HELPING YOUR CHILDREN

see if it can be handled in the judge's chambers, through a court–appointed psychologist, or via videotape. Don't force a courtroom confrontation, which will compel the children to testify for or against one of their parents.

Keep communication lines open between you and the other parent. Keep all discussions of changes in arrangements and money issues between the parents. Don't pass messages through the children. Try to have these discussions over the phone, when the kids are not around. That way, if they become unavoidably heated, your children will not be observers. Don't wait until the other parent comes to pick up or drop off the children to say, "Oh, by the way . . ." This leads to disagreements, which the children can't help but witness.

When the children are back with you, encourage them to talk about their time with the other parent, unless you find that you cannot listen without reacting. Don't pump them for specific information, such as dating relationships, or how the other parent is spending money. You know the motivation behind these questions, and you also know what that information does to you. Ask, "Did you guys have a good time with your father this weekend?" Then be prepared to bite your tongue when they talk about how much fun it was, or even how nice his new girlfriend is. This is extremely difficult for you, but for the sake of your children, encourage their honest expression of this significant part of their lives.

If you find that you cannot listen without reacting, then be honest enough with your children to say, "It hurts me to hear this right now. I want you to have fun with your dad, and maybe someday we will be able to talk all about it. But, for right now, we shouldn't." Then find ways to work on your own adjustment so that later you can encourage your children to share all areas of their lives, especially their relationship with the other parent, and perhaps a stepparent.

Both parents should set aside time alone with each child. This gives them opportunity to create special bonds, and to talk on a deeper level than is possible when all the children are constantly together. This has proven to be an important factor in building a strong sense of security and a healthy self image.

Avoid being a Disneyland Daddy or a Magic Mountain Mommy. Parents who normally do not live with the children tend to avoid the typical patterns of a realistic home environment. They want to make sure the children have a good time when they come to visit. They may eat out frequently, do special things at every visit, and give in on the rules regarding bedtime, homework, etc. In order to decrease instability and competition between the parents, each should strive to provide the same stable and consistent discipline that is expected of the custodial parent. Although special events are nice, the majority of the time should be part of a daily routine, similar to what the children do in the other home. Avoid presents or treats, which seem like relationship bribes. Focus on building the relationship with your children through open communication and time spent doing everyday tasks.

All the children need to feel the continued love of both parents. They need to know that each parent encourages their relationship with the other. Ready access to the departed parent, by phone and in person, is necessary. *You* will benefit if you help your children accept and love the other parent, even when the other parent doesn't do the same.

# CHILD SUPPORT AND ALIMONY

I am not going to say whether or not you should receive alimony, or how much child support you should get. You need to have that discussion with your lawyer or mediator. Rather, let's discuss how these payments (actually, the lack of these payments) affect your children. All fathers (assuming Dad is the noncustodial parent) should make child support payments on time. If there is alimony due, it should be paid on time also. In reality, we know that not all payments are on time, and that many fathers make no payments at all. Whenever this occurs, the children inevitably are affected.

Unless the father is unemployed or on the verge

of bankruptcy, his resistance to keep his financial obligation is usually the result of unresolved anger or resentment toward the mother. Even though the father promises he loves his children, he may resist fulfilling his obligation toward them in order to make a point. Unfortunately, the children suffer because of this decision. Not only are their financial needs being neglected, but the father is contributing to a hostile home atmosphere for the children. Their mother is placed under undue strain, and inevitably will tell the children, "I'm sorry I can't get you those sneakers, because your father hasn't sent the support check."

Witholding payments often is the result of a conflict over visitation. The father tells me he is not going to pay, because his former spouse does not send the children when she is supposed to. Predictably, the mother then tells me that she doesn't send the kids on time, because of the father's sporadic payments. This neverending catch-22 has no winners, and the children end up suffering the most. For the sake of your children, *don't do it!*

Child support and alimony are legal obligations, and have nothing to do with your children. You need to fulfill your obligations, regardless of your relationship with your children or your former spouse. If you are not happy with the arrangement, then take it up with the other parent privately. If that does not resolve your concerns, then go to your lawyer or mediator. Don't resort to punishing your children for your inability to get along with their mother.

On the other hand, mothers, just because your former spouse doesn't make their payments on time, or doesn't even make them at all, you have no right to block their relationship with their children. The same principles apply. The father's visitation rights are a legal obligation, and are critical to your children's healthy adjustment to divorce (assuming he is not abusive). His nonpayment must be taken up with him first, and then approach legal authorities. Fortunately, the courts are beginning to take these matters more seriously, and have started cracking down.

What do we tell the children? In the beginning, say as little as possible. Children, and even teens, should be kept out of financial arrangements and disagreements. However, when the problem persists, such as when no payment has been made in several months, then you may have to tell the children the truth. Let them know that you don't want them to get involved in the dispute, but that "because your father has not made several payments, we will all have to tighten our belts a bit." Let them know that you want them to continue having a good relationship with their father.

I know this advice is hard to swallow when you're in the middle of a financial crisis, or when you can't begin to see any redeeming qualities in the other parent. Let me remind you of the long–term effects of divorce on children, and once again point out that a continued relationship with both parents is crucial to the psychological well–being of your children. Try to focus on these points: "What is the underlying issue in this dispute? How can I resolve this without putting my children in the middle?"

# YOUR CHILDREN AND THE SCHOOL

Mrs. Graham didn't want the school to find out her husband had left. She had her children, Martha and Michael, in a private Christian school. She was afraid that the school's conservative philosophy would prejudice the teachers and administrators against her children. Or if teachers knew, they would watch her children too closely, and look for trouble in her kids.

The problem with Mrs. Graham's cautious attitude is that her fears are unfounded, and may be depriving the children of significant help. As a school psychologist, I consulted with teachers and principals in over twenty public and private schools. It was my experience that teachers were sensitive and compassionate when they became aware of a student's struggles. They were harder on children when they started falling behind or missing assignments with no apparent reason. But in the case of divorce, teachers would make allowances for the children's distractibility, academic regression, emotional withdrawal, or hostility.

Teachers have a variety of resources available to them to help children. Books, tapes, videos, and counselors are usually at the disposal of your children, as long as the school is aware of your need. The school might be holding support groups for children of divorce, or know where they are being held in your community. The bottom line is that you won't know this unless you inform the school of what is going on at home.

If your children are teenagers, probably they have a variety of teachers, and most likely would not appreciate your contacting all of them. In this case, a call to the guidance counselor or advisor may be most helpful. If it is a large school, there is little the counselor will probably do unless they have a special program, or unless your children come in for help. Older children are more influenced by their peer group, and will tend to talk with friends far more than they will talk with teachers or a counselor. Encourage peer interaction, especially with other children who have been through divorce. They can become a tremendous help to each other. (This is a major premise of the Kids in the Middle programs that we conduct—kids helping other kids.) You may need to correct distorted peer feedback from time to time, especially if your children's friends are immature or hostile. Try to be aware of the kinds of support your children are receiving from other kids.

# CHANGES AT HOME

When my family got a divorce, my whole world changed forever. We moved to a new home, a new school district, a new church, and all new friends. I don't know what hurt the most—missing my dad, or missing my friends from my old neighborhood and school.

This quote from an eleven–year–old girl illustrates children's need for stability amid turmoil. There will always be changes to face. Some of these changes may even be good, especially over the long–term. Yet when separation or divorce first occurs, it is helpful if you can keep the changes to a minimum. If you have to move, try to stay in the same school district, or the same social group. Your friendships may evolve toward more single people and fewer married couples, but try to make this transition gradual and smooth.

As parents get together in singles groups and social clubs, it is inevitable that the children will socialize as well. This can result in positive relationships with other kids who have been through similar life changes. This reinforces the fact that "I am not alone," and allows the children opportunity to talk to other kids about their concerns. As a parent, you can't push these new friendships too quickly. Encourage your children to continue their long–term friendships, while allowing new relationships to develop naturally.

Keep the household schedule, responsibilities, and discipline as consistent as possible. If you did not work before, and now have to work, your schedule obviously will change. Sit down with your children, explain the need for the changes, and then let them know what they can expect for the future. It is most important for your children to know you want to be with them, you want to care for them, but the changes force everyone to take on more responsibilities. You might say something like this:

> I have to go back to work in order to help pay the bills. This means I won't be here when you get home from school. I would love to be here for you, fix your snack, and hear all about your day. But unfortunately you'll have to wait until I get home at 5:30. That means you'll have to fix your own snack, and you may even need to help set the table before I get home. What's important is that we work together and make our relationship even stronger than it was before.

Here are a few additional guidelines, which should help you handle the changes at home.

Although increased responsibilities are inevitable, don't allow your kids to become hyper-responsible, taking on burdens and chores they should not shoulder. Let your children remain children. No matter how mature they act, don't fool yourself into believing they can take on adult responsibilities. Boys particularly are susceptible to thinking, "Now that I'm the man of the house, I need to be here for Mom." One boy told me how he could not go away to school in the fall because his mom was going through a difficult time and would need a man around the house.

It is important that parents avoid confiding in their children as if they were peers. This can happen when mothers talk to their daughters about "what a tough life it is out there," or when Dad tells his son all about the women he's dating. Let your child remain a child.

As a parent, you want a close relationship with your children, but there must be some boundaries in that relationship. If you have a problem with setting limits and boundaries in relationships, or grew up in a home where boundaries were confused, then you may be passing this on to your children unconsciously. If this is the case, I encourage you to seek counseling, so that you can create a healthier balance for your children.

Don't force your children to make choices that will create loyalty conflicts for them. For example, don't ask your children, "Whom do you want to spend your birthday with, your mom or your dad?" This creates a no–win situation for your children. If they pick you, they hurt the other parent. And how can they tell you they'd rather be with the other parent? It would be best to get their input by asking a neutral question like,

"How would you like to spend the holiday?" If they neglect the other parent, you may want to suggest a compromise that includes both parents. This approach demonstrates you are sincere in your desire that they have a good relationship with the other parent, and discourages the children's tendency to tell you what they think you want to hear.

Encourage your children to keep their fond memories of the other parent. Many times, on separation, parents do a clean sweep of the house, throwing away all pictures or mementos that remind them of the other parent. Try to save a photo album or two for your children, which will remind them of good times together. A special picture or memento beside their bed or in a wallet should also be suggested. Remember, if you suggest it, this gives the children permission to love the other parent. If you don't suggest it, your children may assume, "Mom would hit the roof if she saw a picture of *him* around."

# SPECIAL FRIENDS AND STEPPARENTS

When one is trying to restructure the family, adding a new "friend" or a stepparent to the system is like throwing a monkey wrench into the works. These additions generally cause a whole new set of adjustments, which take years to work through. If this happens while children are still adjusting to the trauma of divorce, generally within the first two years, all of the emotions can be intensified and acceptance can be much farther away. Many therapists recommend that newly divorced people not get involved in intimate relationships for at least two years following their divorce. This not only helps you to make your adjustment to the divorce, but helps your children also.

This does not mean that you should avoid new friendships with the opposite sex. On the contrary, these relationships, assuming they are healthy, are vital to your recovery. (See the appendix on relationships.) What you need to avoid is committed relationships with the opposite sex, and emotional entanglements that complicate the recovery process for you and your children. These rebound relationships rarely last, and most often lead to more pain for everybody involved. Statistics on remarriage show that when someone remarries within two years of their divorce, they have a greater than 80 percent chance of going through another divorce. Do you or your children need that? For those who wait two years, the odds of making a successful remarriage increase to about 50 percent, which is the same percentage as for first-time marriages.

Your reaction may be, "That's fine for me, but try telling that to the other parent. They're already involved with someone else, and we're not even divorced yet!" Unfortunately, reality dictates that your divorce was probably exacerbated by the involvement of another individual. Now, what do you do?

Many parents use the illicit affair as an excuse to keep the children away from the other parent. I do not condone the relationship, and I understand the depth of your resentment and jealousy. But I must defer to the greater good of your children. As one kid in the middle put it:

> My dad left my mom to live with his girlfriend. When Dad asked if he could pick us up for a visit, Mom refused to let us go over, because she didn't agree with his lifestyle. We knew that what my dad had done was wrong, and in many ways we were really ticked at him. But he was still our father, and we still loved him. Mom not letting us go only created a bunch of mudslinging between my parents. I think I would have respected Mom a lot more if she had told us how she felt, and then allowed us to see him. Now my dad is married to his girlfriend, and our relationship is still strained. I don't want to do it, but sometimes I blame my mom for the fact that I don't really have a relationship with my dad.

Unfortunately, dating relationships have a way of becoming a battleground in the postdivorce experience. Besides being used as an excuse for curtailing visitation, other pitfalls exist for your children as you move toward that special relationship. Here are a few guidelines as you seek to include opposite–sex relationships in your restructured family.

As the noncustodial parent, it would be best if you did most of your socializing on weekends when you do not have the children. Parenting must be your first priority. Particularly in the first few years of your restructured family, you need to give your children as much of your time as possible. Your dates generally will be viewed as intrusions into your relationship with your children. As one particular person becomes important, you will want to introduce that person into your children's lives in a gradual, nonthreatening way.

It is probably much harder for the custodial parent to have a social life. Some potential dates may be scared off by your children. And then there is the problem of the time and energy that it takes to maintain a social life. When the opportunity arises, you should not feel guilty about getting a babysitter, and enjoying a night out. Balance is needed between your right to privacy and your need to be honest with the kids. Your children don't need to meet and approve of everyone you go out with, but you should not hide the fact that you are dating. Your children's trust is built when you are honest with them, even though they may not like your going out without them. Expect some jealousy of your time and attention.

Don't encourage your casual dates to get close to your children. A positive male role model is *not* a series of men that you happen to date. This only confuses your children and reinforces the fact that relationships are not permanent. This adds to their insecurity. While teens are more understanding of temporary relationships, they are not helped by your pushing your new "friends" on them. Integrate your opposite–sex friends into your children's lives only as they become an important part of yours. Allow the relationship to develop at its own pace, never pushing your children into artificial acceptance.

Avoid the temptation to ask your children about the other parent's new friends. This puts your children in the position of spying, and creates loyalty conflicts. If they volunteer the information, try to show little reaction. Encourage your children to treat your friends, and your ex-spouse's friends, with respect. Don't allow the dating relationship to become a source of conflict.

If your children ask you questions about your dating relationships, give them honest answers without personal details. Answer as honestly as you can without giving information about the depth of your relationship, or your plans for the future. That should wait until you are ready to take definite steps.

If your children ask specific questions about your physical relationship, you should answer honestly without making a big deal out of it. Give no details, however.

Once these relationships progress to a point where it looks like remarriage is imminent, you need to have a discussion with your children similar to the one outlined in chapter 8, when you were contemplating separation or divorce. Out of courtesy to your former mate, you may want to forewarn them before you tell the kids, so that they can begin to prepare themselves emotionally. Let's face it, remarriage of either spouse is a difficult transition for both children and parents.

Psychologically speaking, this is a big hurdle for the children. It ends the fantasy that the parents might get back together, triggers the fear that the new spouse will take away parental love, and creates anxiety about whether or not the children will get along with this intruder in the family.

For the parent getting married, it finally closes one chapter in their life, and opens the door of new challenges and opportunities. For the parent remaining single, there is the feeling of being left behind, the anxiety of wondering, "Will I ever be able to move on like that?"

As everyone makes the necessary adjustments, the anxiety which grips your children is the feeling, "Now that Dad has a new wife, he will have even less love and less time for me." This can be particularly threatening if the new marriage includes children. The blending of families is filled with so many complexities that it needs to be the subject of another book. For our purposes, a general review is in order.

In the '90s, one–third of all children will spend at least some time with a stepparent before their eighteenth birthday. It is estimated that by the year 2000, the blended family will be the most common type of family in this country. Yet researchers estimate that it takes an average of five years to blend a family successfully. For most of you getting remarried, your children probably will move out of the house before the necessary transitions are completed.

I have two close friends who were both in long–term relationships that were moving toward marriage. They both chose to postpone their decision because they had teenagers at home. Rather than go through the difficulties of blending a family, both couples decided to wait until the children were out of the house before they got remarried. I'm not saying that you should do the same. I merely want to point out that blending is more difficult than most people realize. One of my friends explained their decision this way.

> I know of over twenty remarried couples, all with teenagers in their blended families. I can't name one family who hasn't had major difficulties with their children after the marriage. I just decided that I didn't want to do that to my kids, so I've postponed my own remarriage for another two years. By then my youngest will leave for college.

A mother of a blended family described the following interaction between her teenage son and her new husband.

Before I married Jim, he and my son Paul were like best friends. I was so excited because I thought that now, after thirteen years of being by ourselves, Paul was going to have a father figure. The strangest thing happened, though. As soon as we got back from the honeymoon, I noticed my son acting a little strange around Jim. Within a few weeks, they were barely speaking. And now, after three years of marriage, Paul and Jim can't even look at each other without getting in a fight. I don't know what happened when Jim and I married, but something obviously clicked off for my son.

This example is not unlike many of the stories I have heard from stepparents, who are horrified by what happens when they try to blend a family. It never seems to be easy. The way everyone gets along before the wedding does not seem to be a very good indication of what to expect afterward. In fact, it is not unusual for the children to push you toward marrying Mr. So-and-so, and then create havoc after the wedding, saying they never really liked him.

If you are thinking about remarriage, I would recommend getting a book that deals specifically with remarriage and stepparenting issues. (See the appendix.) For a general review of some of the issues you will face, here are a few guidelines.

The potential stepparent needs to be introduced to the children in a gradual and natural way. In the beginning, fun outings are best, since they reduce the tension of making conversation. Once the initial transitions are over, natural family activities are best.

Don't expect instant rapport between your children and the new stepparent. These relationships take time, usually many years. If the relationship seems to go well from the beginning, expect a strained transition later.

Younger children usually adjust more quickly to a stepparent than do older children and teenagers.

The stepparent should try to observe family customs and transitions, including giving the children gifts on special occasions. Be careful not to overdo the gift–giving, since children will tend to view this as a bribe.

Don't push your children to participate in your wedding. They may feel intense pressure to be loyal to the other parent. Let them know of your plans. Tell them you would like for them to take part, but you will let them decide for themselves. Then give them several weeks, if possible, to decide.

If the new stepparent does not have children, they need to educate themselves about childhood development and parenting. Don't assume it will come naturally. You are taking on a big commitment, and need to prepare yourself.

Don't expect your children to love or respect their stepparent as much as they do their biological parent. This is unrealistic, and sets up the stepparent for tremendous disappointment.

Don't force your children to call the new stepparent Mom or Dad. Find out what they would prefer, and then try to compromise on a name or nickname that is acceptable to everyone, including your former spouse. (Yes, even after your remarriage, the lines of communication need to stay open.)

Continue to spend individual time with each of your children, and constantly remind them of your undiminished love for them. Keep in mind the childhood fantasy that with each new person or child in your life, you will have less love for them. This is particularly strong if there are stepchildren about the same age as your own children, or if there is a new baby born into the blended family.

While your children need to respect and listen to your new spouse, you need to remain their primary disciplinarian. Younger children can take correction from their stepparent more easily than older children and teenagers. It is unfair to the stepparent for you to expect them to take on the major disciplinary role.

Children generally try to play one parent against the other, but this is particularly intense in a stepparent relationship. Try not to get sucked into this divide–and–conquer strategy. Avoid taking sides with your children or your spouse. Instead, discuss the matter privately with your spouse, and then tell the children your decision.

Remember, they will take it best if it comes from you, their parent.

It is important for you and the stepparent to keep in mind that intense feelings of anger and resentment are normal in the blended family, especially among teenagers. Try not to personalize the anger, and never respond in kind. You are probably bearing the brunt of years of perceived betrayal and disappointment. Be as patient and compassionate as you can be, knowing this is a very difficult transition for everyone.

If you are parenting as a single, and your former spouse is remarrying, you will also have adjustments to make. These adjustments will be in your own attitudes, and with your children, as they report their feelings toward the new person in their lives. It is probably a no–win situation for you. If they love their new stepparent, you will feel replaced; if they don't like their new stepparent, you will have to hear complaints.

Here are a few guidelines intended to help you and your children cope with these changes.

If you can't be accepting of your former spouse's remarriage, at least try to stay as neutral and emotionally uninvolved as possible. If you are really struggling with the whole issue, you probably need to talk with a counselor or advisor about your feelings. It will affect your children's adjustment if you continue to have strong feelings about these changes.

Give your children permission to attend, or

participate in, the wedding. Forbidding them will only hurt their relationship with *you*.

As hard as it might be for you to accept, you need to have an amicable relationship with your former mate's new spouse. You will probably need to talk on the phone from time to time, and it really doesn't help the children if they see you snarling at each other every time you speak.

Give your children permission to talk about the times they spend at the other parent's house. Listen to their stories about the other partner and the other children, but try not to make any judgments, or offer your opinion. Try to remain detached when they complain about, or praise, the stepparent. Stay out of what goes on in the other household, unless you have good reason for significant concern, such as comments like, "They don't feed us over there." Even then, don't assume that it's true. Try to take it up calmly with your former spouse. Only involve the stepparent if you find that you get along better with him or her than you do with your ex–spouse.

# CHAPTER SUMMARY

In this chapter we have looked at some common areas of contention for single parents, and then presented some practical guidelines for helping your children over some of these difficult hurdles. The following is a brief summary of these guidelines:

| INCREASES IMPACT OF DIVORCE | LESSENS IMPACT OF DIVORCE |
|---|---|
| 1. Children involved in visitation and custody squabbles. | 1. Parents work out custody and visitation arrangements cooperatively. |
| 2. Children asked to choose between parents. | 2. Parents help children avoid loyalty conflicts by encouraging relationship with other parent. |
| 3. Parents use children to send messages. | 3. Parents keep lines of communication open. |
| 4. Parents become too busy or distracted. | 4. Parents spend quality time with each child. |
| 5. Parents use children and money as leverage to get what they want. | 5. Parents keep money issues separate from children. |
| 6. Parents isolate | 6. Parents seek |

themselves and their children.

resources and support from a variety of settings, including church, school, family.

7. Parents expect children to take the place of missing parent.

7. Children remain children, even though increased responsibilities may be necessary.

8. Parents deny feelings and do not facilitate discussion with children.

8. Parents allow children to grieve.

9. Parents push children into relationships with a series of dating partners.

9. Parents provide stable adult relationships with relatives and family friends.

10. Remarriage takes place before children have had time to adjust to divorce.

10. Give children at least two years of adjustment before bringing potential stepparent into their lives.

11. Parents maintain angry, bitter feelings.

11. Parents recover and move on to healthy new lifestyle.

12. Parents speak

12. Parents show, and

negatively about other parent in front of children.

13. Absent parent loses contact with children.

express, respect for one another.

13. Absent parent maintains consistent contact with children.

# PARENTING AS A SINGLE

As a single parent of two preschool boys, I found my life going through an overwhelming set of changes. At first, I was too depressed to be any good to anyone, including my boys. Later, I determined that I was going to overcome my circumstances. That led me into my superwoman role, where I tried to do everything by myself. I took a full-time job, arranged daycare for the boys, ran the home, and tried to maintain a social life. I wanted to take the place of their missing father. But I was becoming more and more frustrated, and the boys were usually mad at me. What a terrible feeling!

Now I'm just trying to be a decent mother. I no longer need to be superwoman. I don't even have to be good. I'm settling for doing the best I can, and spending whatever time I can with the boys. It's like I wanted 100 percent before, and now I'm settling for 75 percent. But at least I can preserve my sanity this way. And who knows, maybe I'll even enjoy a few days.

—a thirty-two-year-old single mother

Even though the preceding quote seems a little gloomy, it is a fairly accurate portrayal of how most single parents feel at least some of the time. There is a sense that "I can't do it all myself" and "What do I really have to look forward to?" There is no question about it; parenting as a single is an extremely challenging task, especially if you have little or no support from the other parent. Yet I know of many single parents who not only make it on their own, but appear to be happy, fulfilled, and are raising children who are well-adjusted. In this last chapter, we will look at ways to help you become more effective as a single parent— not only at raising your children, but also at enjoying the life that you have.

Two of the keys for successful single-parenting, which we want to focus on in this chapter, are the way that you raise your children, and your own attitude toward your circumstances. In the first half of the chapter we will discuss the parenting keys. Then we will conclude with the ways in which your own attitude toward your circumstances affects the entire single-parenting process.

# KEYS FOR PARENTING AS A SINGLE

*The Fresh Start Single-Parenting Workbook* focuses on healthy parenting skills for the single parent. What I will focus on in this section is an overview of the issues. In addition, I will provide a list of other resources, which might be helpful to you if you would like to look more closely at a particular parenting skill.

Parenting as a single is not a whole lot different than parenting in general. Both require loving discipline, guidance, modeling, nurturing, teaching, and a full range of emotional supports. The greatest difference for the single parent is twofold. One, your children tend to be more emotionally needy because of their sense of loss. Two, you don't have the additional support of a second parent with whom you can share your decisions and frustrations. So you need to focus on a few critical skills that you can commit to working on. Here are some of the most important areas.

## Provide a loving environment for your children.

Everyone would agree that providing a loving environment is one of the most important gifts you can give to your children. But many would disagree as to what a loving environment entails. Should we be firm or compassionate, foster independence or reliance on the family, give in to their wishes or force them to do without? These are all questions that have different answers, depending on the circumstances and the personality of your children. The important point is that you assure your children of your unconditional love for them.

Unconditional love for children of divorce must come in the form of constant reassurance of your love and commitment to their well–being. They need to know you will be there for them, and they are a top priority, even though you have additional responsibilities which require your time. They need to see concrete expressions of that love during good times and bad.

Practical expressions of love should include the following:

- Verbal reassurance of specific things that you like about each child.
- Physical contact with your children, which includes hugs, kisses, back scratches, etc. (I still remember my mom waking me up on school days by gently scratching my back.)
- Notes and cards, which express pleasure with something they have done, or something you like about their personality. (This is particularly helpful for the noncustodial parent to do.)
- Spend individual time with each child. Find a hobby or activity you can share with them alone.
- Actively listen to your child. Focus on them

and what they are saying. Stop what you are doing and give them good eye contact. Do not give advice, or simplistic answers, but try to view the information through their eyes.

- For the noncustodial parent, make frequent phone calls during the week, which focus on them and their day. Also, give them a number where you can be reached at almost any time. They need to be assured that they have easy access to you when they feel they need to talk about something.

No one is capable of displaying unconditional love at all times. However, if this is your goal, then you need also to be able to ask for forgiveness when you fail with your kids. If you grew up in a home that was less than loving, then you might have particular difficulty expressing this love to your children. For a more in–depth look at learning how to love your children, I would recommend the following books: *How to Really Love Your Child* by Ross Campbell, *The Art of Loving* by Eric Fromm, and *Unconditional Love* by John Powell.

### Rebuild trusting relationships.

One of the casualties of divorce is the ability to trust again, at least immediately. This is just as true for children as it is for adults. As a parent, it is primarily your responsibility to rebuild your children's trust, since you are probably the most influential adult in their lives. You may also be the target of their distrust, if you were the one who left, or if you are perceived as having betrayed the family in some way.

Rebuilding trust takes time. Above all, it requires complete honesty from you. This is demonstrated in the way you explain divorce to your children, whether or not you are willing to admit your own mistakes, how honest you are with your feelings, and whether or not you keep promises to the children. In an effort to compensate children for losses experienced in divorce, some parents compound the mistake by making promises to the children that they are not sure they can keep. Vacations and extravagant toys do not tell the children you love them. More often than not, they are reinforcement of the belief that Mom or Dad can't be trusted.

Even if you got away with minor unfulfilled promises before the divorce, what you must realize is that now your life is under a microscope. Your children are testing to see if they can trust you again. You must take special care to measure your words before you speak.

These promises include the negative ones, too. If you tell your children, "If I hear you whine one more time, I'll send you to your room for a month." Don't say it unless you can follow through. This might seem like a minor infraction, for which we have all been guilty. But now, more than ever, it is imperative that you think before you speak.

Consider the following statements: "If you do that one more time, I'll kill you!" "If you don't clean up your plate, you won't eat for a week." "If you don't get in the car right now, I'll never take you to Grandma's again."

Besides the fact that you shouldn't make such harsh statements, think about the message these words convey to your children regarding their ability to trust you again. I know we've all sent these messages, or not followed through on a commitment merely because it slipped our minds. When we become aware of these mistakes, it is important that we speak the truth as lovingly as we can.

You might say something like this: "I'm sorry I said that. Mommy didn't really mean that she wouldn't feed you for a week. I only said that out of frustration. You need to finish your meal, or you won't get any dessert." Or, "I know Daddy said he would take you fishing this weekend, but I forgot that I had to get the car inspected. It was my fault for not remembering. I know you're disappointed, but I'm sure we will be able to go some other time. How about if we try . . ."

### Provide firm, yet loving discipline.

Another casualty in many divorcing families is a continued level of loving discipline. As you lose touch with your children, or lose the energy to keep up with their immaturity, many parents take the easy way out, which is to give in or react in haste. Yet consistent discipline is key to the children of divorce feeling secure and loved.

It is not within the scope of this book to cover the full range of disciplining techniques. I will review a few guidelines, and then recommend some books.

*Make the punishment fit the crime.* This takes a great deal of wisdom, and no one can be there to tell you how to handle each new situation. But don't overreact to minor infractions, and take seriously the mistakes that carry long–term implications. The way this is played out in many homes is for parents to let things slide until they've had enough. Then they react with the back of their hand, or a threat that everyone knows they will not follow through on. Logical consequences make the most sense, and also teach valuable lessons.

"If you don't put away your toys, I'll have to take them away for a couple of days." "If you don't turn off the Nintendo now, you won't be allowed to play with it tomorrow." "Since I don't like to see you act that way, why don't you sit in the other room until you're done pouting?"

The consequences to each situation require thought and patience. This means you need to stay calm, and not react in anger. The easiest thing to do is not always the best.

*Pick your battlegrounds.* You need to decide which areas are important enough to battle over. This is particularly true of teenagers. Since discipline takes a lot of thought and energy, you may decide not to fight over cleaning up every bite on the plate, or whether your daughter can wear makeup to school. You need to decide in advance which issues are important, and on which you need to show some latitude.

*Distinguish among accidents, disobedience, and defiance.* Even though accidents may be devastating to you personally, you don't want to deal with them as harshly as disobedience or defiance. For example, if my daughter spills her juice on my computer and ruins it, I'm going to be very upset. (Especially if I'm at the end of a chapter that I haven't saved to the disk yet.) Her seeing how upset I am may be punishment enough. In fact, I'd probably end up hugging her and assuring her, "It's okay, I realize it was an accident."

But if I tell her to sit in the kitchen and drink her juice, and instead she walks into my office and spills her juice, now I need to punish her for disobedience. Perhaps sitting her in her chair for a while would be sufficient penance, even though my anger at the moment might tempt me to do more.

The most serious infraction is defiance. This is evidenced by my daughter looking me right in the eye and pouring the juice on my computer, right after I told her to take her juice back to the kitchen. For this, a young child could be restricted to her room. An older child might have to work in order to replace the computer they ruined, which would be a logical consequence of their action.

As you can see from the example, the result is the same. My computer is ruined. The difference, which needs to be distinguished, is, was it an accident, disobedience, or defiance?

*Explain to your children the difference between your feelings toward them and your feelings about their behavior.* In other words, tell your children, "I love you, but I don't like the way you are behaving."

Remember when your parents used to say just before they spanked you, "This is going to hurt me more than it will hurt you"? Even though that used to drive us crazy at the time, the message behind the words is, "Because I love you, I have to do this. But it hurts me, too."

Think about the following statements, and how they should be said.

"You're stupid," might become, "I know you are very capable, but the way you're acting right now isn't very smart."

"Shut up!" could be stated, "I want to listen to you, but could you please stop talking right now so that I can think?"

"I hate it when you do that!" might need the minor modification to, "I love you, but I don't like it when you do that."

These changes seem obvious in the calm reality of the present, but they take great willpower and thought when you reach the height of your frustration. I guess that's why people say, "Parenting is hard work!"

Some books that take a closer look at issues of disciplining your children are *Dare to Discipline*, *The Strong-Willed Child* by James Dobson, and *The Key To Your Child's Heart* by Gary Smalley.

### Foster healthy relationships.

As a single parent it is very important that you promote healthy role models for your children. These usually include monitoring whom they hang out with, finding positive opposite-sex and same-sex adult relationships, and providing exposure to healthy, intact families. Here are a few guidelines to help you accomplish this.

*Insist on meeting your children's friends.* Even if they are teenagers, you are entitled to know whom your children are hanging around with. Try to be friendly and open-minded toward all of them. Be cautious about disapproving of any of their friends, since this can make the relationship even more important. Remember, you can't pick your children's friends. Even to suggest a person can sometimes be the kiss of death for that relationship. Usually, the most you can do is to put your children in places where they will be in close proximity to more desirable peer groups; such as church, the YMCA, clubs, civic groups.

*Find adult role models for your children who will be a stable and reliable influence.* This is especially important if your former mate does not provide that type of support. If the other parent is not very involved with your children, then a role model of the opposite sex is critical. This should be a family friend, a grandparent, an uncle—someone whom they can count on to be there for them over the long haul. This is not a series of boyfriends or girlfriends who might be in and out of your life.

If it is a friend, then it is best when the person is interested primarily in helping your children, and not trying to get closer to you. If no one has shown real interest in fulfilling this role, you might want specifically to ask a friend or relative to help out. They might not realize the need, and would be flattered that you turned to them.

*Maintain relationships with some healthy married couples.* Even though many of your friendships will evolve away from married couples and toward singles, it is important that you and your children observe some happily married couples, so that you don't lose your perspective. One teenager recently told me, "I don't know if I'll ever get married. I don't know of a single family where there hasn't been a divorce, or one that isn't headed in that direction."

Another girl told me, "I'm really nervous around men. I've never lived in a home with a man, because my dad left when I was three.

Whenever I'm around couples, I always check out the husband and wife to see how they act. I want to know what a normal family looks like for when I get married; that is, if that ever happens."

Times with relatives and friends who are married, both during holidays and when they're just doing their daily routine, can be a very important part of your children's development.

## Build a positive sense of self-worth.

No matter what your job, your most important responsibility is raising your children. And probably one of the greatest gifts you can pass on to your children is a balanced self-image. Of all of the problems I face in counseling, and in day-to-day contact with people, the most prevalent and pervasive are those of insecurity and poor self-image. To some extent, we all struggle with these from time to time.

Each of us must ask, "What does our society value in a person? What values do I reinforce in my home?" Unfortunately, in most settings, children see that they are valued primarily in four areas: beauty, brains, brawn, and bucks. Our society reflects these values in everything from advertising and cartoons, to who gets elected to the local school board or women's club.

If children are not good-looking or smart, they often feel like failures and may be treated that way by classmates. This is particularly true for girls, who must look like a Barbie Doll.

Boys can get away with not being exceptionally handsome or smart, as long as they are good at sports, or are among the strongest kids in the class.

You may be surprised at how important money is to children's popularity and standing with peers. Our children must wear the right clothes, have the latest games and toys, and even have the correct label on their sneakers. Children are also keenly aware of who lives in the right neighborhoods, and whose parents are influential in the community.

If children do not have at least one of the four ingredients—beauty, brains, brawn, or bucks—then they are destined to an uphill struggle in order to achieve acceptance in our society. One difficult truth, which complicates this problem, is that no matter how blessed we may be, there is always someone out there who is a little prettier, smarter, stronger, or richer. No matter how many of the ingredients we do have, we will still struggle from time to time with a negative self–image.

Given these difficulties, how can I help to develop a positive self–image in my children? Let me describe briefly some general guidelines, and then recommend a few books which expand on this topic.

*You need to love yourself before you can love others.* If you do not have a good self–image, then your first task is to get help for yourself, so that you can model a positive self–image for your children.

*You need to counterbalance what their peer group values.* When your children are with you, you need to show them a more secure kind of love. This is a love not based on how they look or act, but one that values and loves them all the time. Show them love that is unconditional.

*Nurture your children with physical attention and concrete expressions of love.* Be sure to mention specific things that you like about each child.

*Encourage your children to be open and honest with their feelings.* Don't negate their feelings, even when you disagree with them. You need to be an example of open and honest communication.

*Foster independence in your children.* Remember, your goal is not to create obedient clones, but responsible adults. You must encourage their decision-making and willingness to try things on their own, even when you think it might lead to failure. When they do fail, allow them to suffer the consequences, but then be there for them emotionally, encouraging them to try again.

Some additional guidelines can be found in the following books: *How to Really Love Your Child* by Ross Campbell, *Hide and Seek* by James Dobson, *The Key to Your Child's Heart* by Trent and Smalley, and *Raising Positive Kids in a Negative World* by Zig Ziglar.

## *Give your children a sense of purpose or meaning in their lives.*

This is a parenting skill that is vastly over-looked, and yet is critically important for your children's healthy development. Children and adults need to have something in their lives that gives them meaning and purpose. For some it is their work, for others it may be in serving society, while others seek a personal relationship with God. Whatever your priority, you have probably come to find that living solely for self is an unful-filling quest. Many have found greater fulfillment when they live for something beyond themselves.

One of the failures of the yuppie generation was their pursuit of wealth and power, devoid of ethical considerations. King Solomon, one of the richest and most powerful men of his time, said, "All that the world has to offer is a vain pursuit." As we teach our children how to make their way in this world, we must not forget that a faith or belief system should be part of the fabric of our lives.

I hear many parents almost apologize for what they believe. This sends a message to our children about how important our moral values are to us. Many don't want to offend others. But with our children, we have an obligation to present a firm set of values, which tell us who we are and why we are here. Young children will not understand these concepts, and teenagers will rebel against them, so many parents ask, "Why bother?" The answer is one you have heard before. Children may not understand it now, or may not want to hear it later, but the seeds you plant today will have a big influence on how they live as adults. Solomon put it this way in the book of Proverbs: "Train up a child in the way he should go, and when he is old, he will not depart from it."

There are many things you will want to teach your children as they grow up. The best way to teach a belief system, or your faith, is to live it. You don't want to preach it without living it. That would only create an opposite reaction. If you don't have meaning or purpose in your own life, that needs to be settled first. For this, I recommend the book *Power for Living* by Jamie Buckingham.

## YOUR ATTITUDE TOWARD YOUR SITUATION

Let's shift the focus from our children to ourselves. We have come full circle in this book. In the first chapter, I mentioned the Serenity Prayer, and how important an attitude of acceptance toward the things that you cannot change can be in your recovery. I went on to discuss the things you can change, and how you can effect positive change for your children. Now, in this final section, we will take a closer look at how your attitude toward your circumstances can affect your entire life.

## HELPING YOUR CHILDREN

The parents' attitude about their situation has a bearing on how they interact with their former spouse, how they relate with their children, and the speed at which their own recovery takes place. Let's contrast two situations.

Both Mrs. A and Mrs. B are suburban housewives. As they were approaching their fortieth birthdays, their husbands left them for younger women. Both women were devastated by the loss, as were their children. Neither women were educated beyond their high school degrees, and neither worked since getting married. Mrs. A views herself as a victim. She is angry with her ex, and boasts about giving him a hard time. She got full legal and physical custody of their three children, along with four years of alimony, so that she could train for some type of new career. Currently, about two years after her divorce, Mrs. A is working as a receptionist for little more than minimum wage. She has no plans for her vocational education. She says, "I'm really not very good at anything. Besides," she explains, "I never wanted this divorce in the first place. I don't think I should have to work, when I have three kids at home."

Mrs. A has very few social outlets, and many of her married friends are drifting away from her. She is feeling more isolated, and tells her children about how unfair all of this has been for her. Her children feel sorry for her, and feel guilty when they want to visit their dad. He has been sporadic in his visits, and late with many of his payments. But, as he puts it, "At least I'm still there for them when they need me."

Mrs. B, on the other hand, seems to be doing a lot better. She went back to school. Now, two years later, she is well along in completing her business administration degree. She has already started her own small business, doing word processing out of her home. She also has physical custody of her two children, but she and her ex have joint legal custody. Mrs. B requested this arrangement because she knew that her husband would stay more involved in the kids' lives if he had some continuing input into their upbringing. As she put it, "I may not be married to him, but he is still their father. Even though he didn't turn out to be such a good husband, he was always a good father—and I believe he still is."

Mr. B has a good relationship with his children, and they enjoy their visits with him. They feel good about leaving for his place, and good about telling Mom all about their weekends, because they know that their mother encourages this.

Mrs. B is very involved socially. She has found a new support system, with friends who have been through similar life changes. Yet she still stays friendly with one or two of the married couples with whom she was formerly acquainted. Mrs. B describes her life in this way.

> I wouldn't wish divorce on my worst enemy,
> but I wouldn't trade anything for what I have

learned, having gone through a divorce. I have more self–confidence and feel more fulfilled now than I ever have. I never would have thought I could make it on my own while I was married, but now I know I can. I understand more about myself and other people. I think this has made me a better friend to my friends, a better parent to my kids, and a better person. Sure, I get lonely sometimes, but there are worse things than being single and lonely, and one of them is being in a bad marriage. Besides, now I have much stronger friendships, with people whom I know I can count on when I need a listening ear.

In our Fresh Start Seminars, we describe a poster that features a man with a funnel in his head, and a spigot where his nose should be. In the funnel is a bunch of lemons, and out of the spigot, lemonade is pouring into a pitcher. The caption reads, "When life gives you lemons, make lemonade."

This is a perfect illustration of how divorce affects our lives. We have all been given some lemons in our lives. (Some of us married them.) Yet, in spite of these bitter experiences, we still have the ability to choose our own attitude toward our circumstances. Will we choose to become bitter, to squeeze those lemons and serve other people lemon juice? You know what happens when someone serves lemon juice. The sour taste turns people away. We alienate our friends, our children, and even ourselves.

Or will we choose to add some sugar to that lemon juice, and serve lemonade? The sugar, which we all possess, is a sweet disposition, the ability to forgive, to love, and to uplift others. When we add this to the bitter experiences of life, we find a perfect combination of sweet and sour, which attracts others, like lemonade on a hot and thirsty day.

Charles Swindoll, in his book, *Strengthening Your Grip*, explains this concept as follows (pp. 205–206):

> The colorful, nineteenth-century showman and gifted violinist Nicolo Paganini was standing before a packed house, playing through a difficult piece of music. A full orchestra surrounded him with magnificent support. Suddenly one string on his violin snapped and hung gloriously down from his instrument. Beads of perspiration popped out on his forehead. He frowned but continued to play, improvising beautifully.
>
> To the conductor's surprise, a second string broke. And shortly thereafter, a third. Now there were three limp strings dangling from Paganini's violin as the master performer completed the difficult composition on the one remaining string. The audience jumped to its feet and in good Italian fashion, filled the hall with shouts and screams,

"Bravo! Bravo!" As the applause died down, the violinist asked the people to sit back down. Even though they knew there was no way they could expect an encore, they quietly sank back into their seats.

He held the violin high for everyone to see. He nodded at the conductor to begin the encore and then he turned back to the crowd, and with a twinkle in his eye, he smiled and shouted, "Paganini . . . and one string!" After that he placed the single-stringed Stradivarius beneath his chin and played the final piece on *one* string as the audience (and the conductor) shook their heads in silent amazement. "Paganini . . . and one string!" *And*, I might add, an attitude of fortitude.

Dr. Victor Frankl, the bold, courageous Jew who became a prisoner during the Holocaust, endured years of indignity and humiliation by the Nazis before he was finally liberated. At the beginning of his ordeal, he marched into a gestapo courtroom. His captors had taken away his home and family, his cherished freedom, his possessions, even his watch and wedding ring. They had shaved his head and stripped his clothing off his body. There he stood before the German high command, under the glaring lights being interrogated and falsely accused. He was destitute, a helpless pawn in the hands of brutal, prejudiced, sadistic men. He had nothing. No, that isn't true. He suddenly realized there was one thing no one could ever take away from him—just one. Do you know what it was?

Dr. Frankl realized he still had the power to choose his own attitude. No matter what anyone would ever do to him, regardless of what the future held for him, the attitude choice was his to make. Bitterness or forgiveness. To give up or to go on. Hatred or hope. Determination to endure or the paralysis of self-pity. It boiled down to "Frankl . . . and one string!"

Words can never adequately convey the incredible impact of our attitude toward life. The longer I live, the more convinced I become that life is 10 percent what happens to us and 90 percent how we respond to it.

The question remains, "What will *my* attitude be toward *my* circumstances?" Will it be bitterness, self-pity, and immobilization, as with Mrs. A? Or will you choose forgiveness, hope, endurance, and determination, as Mrs. B described? What kind of music are you going to play on that one string of yours?

I know you're thinking, "Yes, but you don't understand how much I've been hurt." Or, "You can't imagine what a creep I was married to." Look again at the life of Victor Frankl. You could not have suffered as much as he did. Are you going to be a victim, or a victor? Before you answer that you'd rather remain in your self-pity, think about your children. Do you want *them* to overcome their circumstances? What attitude would you like for them to choose? Research has demonstrated that the attitude of the parent, especially the custodial parent, is the biggest predictor of the children's adjustment.

The title of this book does not convey the attitude that you and your children need to adopt. Even though you have had some terrible things happen to you as a family, I believe there is still great hope. You *can* serve lemonade, and your children can, too. It's your choice!

# CHAPTER SUMMARY

In our final chapter, we have examined some of the most important keys for parenting as a single. Each parenting key included practical guidelines on how to implement them. These included:

- Provide a loving environment for your children.
- Rebuild trusting relationships.
- Provide firm yet loving discipline.
- Foster healthy relationships.
- Build a positive sense of self–worth.
- Give your children a sense of purpose and meaning to their lives.

In the last section, we discussed the importance of your attitude toward your situation, and how that affects the recovery of you and your children. Your decision to play beautiful music on whatever strings you have left, is the most important gift you can pass on to your children—the truly innocent *victors* over divorce.

# APPENDIX

The following books are recommended readings available from Fresh Start Seminars. They deal with specific issues surrounding divorce and single parenting. Any of these books or tapes can be ordered by calling our office at 1–800–882–2799 during regular business hours (E.S.T.). Please have your VISA or Mastercard ready if you would like to order by phone. Written requests should be sent to: Fresh Start, 63 Chestnut Road, Paoli, PA 19301. (Books marked with an asterisk are highly recommended.)

## Adult Children of Divorce

Brisset and Burns. *The Adult Child of Divorce. Thomas Nelson Publishers, 1991.

Wallerstein, Judith. *Second Chances. Ticknor & Fields, 1989.

# Anger

Lerner, Harriet Goldhor. *Dance of Anger.* Harper & Row, 1985.

# Children's and Teens' Books

Sprague, Gary. *Kids Caught in the Middle: An Interactive Workbook for Children.* Thomas Nelson, 1993.

Sprague, Gary, with Randy Petersen. *Kids Caught in the Middle: An Interactive Workbook for Teens.* Thomas Nelson, 1993.

Sprague, Gary. *My Parents Got a Divorce.* David C. Cook, 1992.

# Codependency

Beattie, Melody. *Beyond Codependency.* Harper & Row, 1987.

————*Codependent No More.* Harper & Row, 1989.

Halpern, Howard. *How To Break Your Addiction to a Person.* Bantam, 1982.

# Depression

Baker and Nester. *Depression.* Multnomah Press, 1983.

Emery, Gary. *Getting Undepressed.* Simon & Schuster, 1988.

Minirth and Meier. *Happiness Is a Choice.* Baker Books, 1978.

# Divorce Recovery

Burns, Bob. *Through The Whirlwind*. Thomas Nelson Publishers, 1989.

Burns and Whiteman. *The Fresh Start Divorce Recovery Workbook*. Thomas Nelson, 1992.

*Fresh Start Tape Series*. Eight 60–minute audio tapes on recovery from divorce.

# Parenting

Campbell, Ross. *How to Really Love Your Child*. Victor Books, 1982.

Dobson, James. *Dare to Discipline*. Tyndale House, 1970.

———*Hide or Seek: Building Your Child's Self–Esteem*. Revell Co., 1979.

———*The Strong–Willed Child*. Tyndale House, 1978.

Smalley, Gary. *The Key to Your Child's Heart*. Thomas Nelson, 1988.

*Whiteman, Thomas. *The Fresh Start Single-Parenting Workbook*. Thomas Nelson, 1993.

Ziglar, Zig. *Raising Positive Kids In a Negative World*. Oliver-Nelson, 1985.

# Relationships

Inrig, Gary. *Quality Friendships*. Moody Press, 1981.

Jones, Tom. *Sex and Love When You're Single Again*. Thomas Nelson Publishers, 1990.

Peck, M. Scott. *The Road Less Traveled*. Simon & Schuster, 1978.

Swindoll, Chuck. *Dropping Your Guard*. Word Books, 1983.

White, Jerry and Mary. *Friends and Friendship*. NavPress, 1982.

## Remarriage

Cerling, Charles. *Remarriage: Opportunity to Grow*. Power Books, 1988.

Frydenger and Frydenger. *The Blended Family*. Zondervan, 1985.

Johnson, Carolyn. *How to Blend a Family*. Zondervan, 1989.

## Separation

Chapman, Gary. *Hope for the Separated*. Moody Press, 1982.

Medved, Diane. *The Case Against Divorce*. Ivy Books, 1990.

## Spiritual Life

Crabb, Larry. *Inside Out*. NavPress, 1988.

Lucado, Max. *No Wonder They Call Him the Savior*. Multnomah Press, 1986.

Swindoll, Charles. *Strengthening Your Grip*. Word Books, 1982.